Pseud Dragon

Tales for Sportsmen

Pseud Dragon

Tales for Sportsmen

ISBN/EAN: 9783742899255

Manufactured in Europe, USA, Canada, Australia, Japa

Cover: Foto ©Thomas Meinert / pixelio.de

Manufactured and distributed by brebook publishing software (www.brebook.com)

Pseud Dragon

Tales for Sportsmen

TALES FOR SPORTSMEN.

By DRAGON.

ILLUSTRATED BY G. BOWERS.

LONDON:
SIMPKIN, MARSHALL, & CO.
1885.

Dedicated

TO ALL TRUE SPORTSMEN OF GREAT BRITAIN

TO WHOM THE

AUTHOR'S GRATEFUL THANKS ARE DUE

FOR MANY PLEASANT DAYS SPENT IN THEIR COMPANY,

AND HIS SENTIMENTS

MAY BE BEST EXPRESSED BY WISHING THEM

IN THE WORDS OF THE OLD TOAST

"LUCK AND AN OPEN SEASON."

PREFACE.

This little collection of tales for sportsmen hardly requires a preface, most of them having already appeared between Baily's green covers and in various weekly sporting papers, but a preface is usually expected, and especially from unknown authors who generally seize the opportunity to disarm, or try at least to disarm, stern or venomous critics by explaining their modest ambition in venturing to publish a book.

It has been an amusement to write these tales, and now that they are brought together with the addition of illustrations by an artist whose well-known pencil needs no comment, if the sportsmen of Great Britain will accept them a gratified author will be almost satisfied. To be thoroughly satisfied depends on the sale, but one word is necessary in offering these stories to the public.

These tales are mostly composed of facts supplemented by fiction, while some may be fiction founded on facts, and the true art of an author is the blending of fact and fiction, so that no one shall know where facts end and fiction begins; therefore if, in the desire to please all parties, an author now and then exceeds the bounds of moderation either way stern critics should be lenient.

CONTENTS.

	PAGE
THE RULING PASSION	3
THE RULING PASSION—SEQUEL	31
SHALL I?	51
THE BITER BIT	67
WITH ROYALTY ON EXMOOR, 1879	75
NOTES ON RIDING TOURS. I.	91
NOTES ON RIDING TOURS. II.	99
BRICKET WOOD	111
RUN OF THE (FESTIVE) SEASON, CHRISTMAS, 1878	129
HUNT SUBSCRIPTIONS	137
A LEGITIMATE SWINDLE	145
DRAG HUNTING	153

LIST OF ILLUSTRATIONS.

"WELL DONE YOU!"		*Frontispiece.*
"WHO-WHOOP! TEAR IT UP!"	*To face page*	24
"YOU ARE IN TROUBLE, LITTLE LADY?"	,, ,,	37
"MISSIS! DOCTOR!!"	,,	58
LIKE A SHOT RABBIT	,, ,,	63
MARCHED HIM OFF IN TRIUMPH	,,	70
AWKWARD WORK	,, ,,	83
OPERATING WITH A BESOM	,, ,,	98
HINT FOR ROAD SURVEYORS	,, ,,	104
"DEAR OLD BRICKET"	,, ,,	122
NO WHIP, NO VOICE, NO HORN!	,, ,,	133
FORTY MILES AN HOUR	,, ,,	149

THE RULING PASSION.

TALES FOR SPORTSMEN.

THE RULING PASSION.

NO keener sportsman ever rode a horse or cheered a hound than John Hardacre, Master of the Ravensdale Harriers. With him hunting was the ruling passion before which everything else must give way. His father had been Master for years, so John had been early entered, and report says his first days with hounds were enjoyed when two years old, strapped in a basket on an old pony led by the feeder. The little chap would clap his hands and crow with delight, seeming to know all about it when hounds found and went away with their merry cry. His mother died when he was quite young, so it need not be said he was idolised by his father, who never married again, but lavished all his love on his only child. Just enough schooling to teach him to read, write, keep accounts, and an insight into general knowledge satisfied his father, and at the age of fourteen he was promoted to the office of whipper-in. Right well he filled the post, to the delight and admiration of the old gentleman, who hunted his own pack, and great was the sport they showed. John was a bold rider and fine horseman, quick as lightning, but quiet and patient; so, under his father's tuition, he quickly learnt all about hunting. A bad fall made it necessary for the old gentleman to give up his horn to his son and take a less active part in the field, and shortly after he joined the majority, deeply regretted by all who knew him, leaving his son a comfortable farm and income, with a pack of twenty couple of 20 inch harriers, second to none in the kingdom.

The pack had been carefully bred for years, and John fully kept up their reputation.

The Ravensdale kennels were situated in a fine hunting country, a good deal of grass, strongly fenced; and, what is all important to a harrier country, there were some high downs, famous for a hardy, flying breed of hares, which would often take to the low country and give their followers some tremendous runs.

At the time of my story, September 187—, John had been Master, showing capital sport, for five years since his father's death, and was twenty-seven years of age. Standing five feet ten, his riding weight eleven stone, just enough, as he said, to steady them without being a burden, he was the *beau idéal* of a horseman. Though well off, he was not a rich man, according to present ideas, so he made his stud pay for their keep. Being a good judge of horseflesh, he always bought a lot of colts at fairs or direct from the breeders, which he would turn out in his meadows; or, if old enough, make them at once, always selling at a considerable profit, either privately or sending the stud to Tattersall's at the end of the season, and being well known, any horse that passed through his hands was safe to fetch a top price. He kept six for his own riding, for besides hunting his own hounds three days a week, often with a second horse out, there were two packs of fox-hounds within reach, so he always went two days a week with one or other. Thursday he never hunted, as it was market-day at the county town, and he always attended to meet his neighbours, transact what business he had to do, and dine with them afterwards, the same as his father had always done. The ordinary, without him to keep it alive would have been a dull affair, he had a joke and merry smile for every one. Wherever he was, his jolly humour seemed to pervade the company, and good fellowship reigned supreme. There were three horses for the whips, and, of course, a Jack-of-all-trades, which is to be found in every hunting establishment, and does more work than all the others put together. No money would ever induce his owner to part with that grey cob, though large sums had often been offered. A tough, wiry old beggar, of any age, standing 14.2, with flat, clean legs, short back, and rare shoulders, he could gallop and jump all day long, with Master or whips, doing all the hacking work besides, and as for harness, he always seemed to be taking his rest between the shafts, either going to the town in the trap, or at a pinch drawing home a fallen comrade to the way of all flesh.

The establishment consisted of the old feeder, John Wilson, who had been with them all his life. His son Joe was now whip, while his son John again was second whip, or second horseman for the Master, as the case might be. So there were three generations in the kennel, all bound to their young Master with almost family ties, serving him with devotion unfortunately rarely seen in these days. Old John, who was a widower, lived with his grandson, for company, close to the kennels, so as to be at hand in case of accident. Joe lived in the house, for, besides being whip, he was stud groom (of course having three or four helpers under him in the stable), butler and valet; and his wife, cook and housekeeper, for the Master was a bachelor, and so far as any one knew not likely to change his state. Though fond of plain living, everything must be of the best, and he kept a good cellar, often giving little sociable dinners to his friends, and it need not be said they were all hunting men.

It was a bright sunny morning, early in October, they were to meet at the kennels for the opening day, and according to custom the Master provided a breakfast, to which all his supporters were made welcome.

The field as a rule numbered about twenty, and there were some good men amongst them, who would hold their own with any company across any country. Eleven o'clock was the time of meeting, and due justice having been done to the plain but ample breakfast, the sport of the day commenced.

It was a pretty sight as the Master rode out from the kennel-yard, surrounded by the merry little pack. Twelve couple, mixed but level, for they kept only the smallest dog-hounds. Well mounted on a well-bred grey, the Master showed off at his best in a new green coat, everything in character, from cap to spurs. A cheery smile lighted up his keen, close-shaved face. Some one asked him once why he did not grow a moustache. "I wear a moustache! How the blazes should I ever clap a horn tight to my lips to blow in a hurry, with one of those darned things frizzling round my mouth?" So he kept his hard, keen face clean shaved, and of course the servants were the same. Like the Master, they were in new green coats; Joe in front on a thoroughbred bay, and his son behind on a rare chestnut, in case his Master wanted a second horse, for he would be with his hounds, and they did not make short days early in the season.

Of the field, the squire of the parish was there to try a new purchase; the parson on a well-bred cob would show most of them the way, and knew more about hunting than a good many; the curate, who had already been his rounds, visiting the poor, and had looked in at the village school, but the boys had begged a holiday, which the master had willingly given, and there they were together on foot, keen as any of the field, surrounded by a bevy of boys all eager for sport. Twelve or fourteen well-mounted farmers, and one or two of the local gentry, with a few grooms on their masters' horses, out for an hour or two's schooling, comprised the field. Just as they were moving off, a young lady on a wiry little bay mare, accompanied by a lad, evidently her brother, on a dun pony, trotted up. "Who's the habit?" said the Master, who hated the sight of them out with hounds, to Joe. "Don't know, sir, but I'll soon find out," and he began his inquiries amongst the field, keeping his eye on the hounds though, all the time, as they began drawing a meadow beneath the churchyard, which, under the parson's care, always held a hare. "Whoop, she goes!" Away they went with a merry cry, and all else was forgotten. "Half-past eleven," says the timekeeper, but no one else bothers about looking at his watch. The Master and Joe sail away with the pack over a good country down to the parson's garden, where the hare has evidently been on visiting terms, and no doubt punished the carnations and parsley bed, but there is no time to linger now, for, while the field stay in the paddock, the hounds bustle her through and the Master's quick eye catches view as she runs down the carriage-drive to the open again. Scent is good, and they fly along down past the school-meadows to the stiffly fenced country beyond, and the field gets select as they drive her at a good pace down to a big brook which has often proved a stopper to a harder riding field. Over she goes with the pack on good terms, and never a bridge within half a mile. The grey is not so good at water as he is at timber, but it is a case of necessity, and that is more than half the battle with a good man on his back.

Fourteen feet of naked water with rotten banks, even at this time of year, takes some doing, so our Master began to ride as soon as he jumped into the field. As he goes best pace at the brook he hears some one alongside and looking over his shoulder.

"Blame me, but it's the habit! what business has she to go at water?"

That last vicious dig did the trick for him though, and landed the grey safely over, while the game little bay mare flew it like a bird. "Well done you," thought our Master; "but you're a trump anyhow. Darned if I like to see a woman risk her neck, though, like that. Forrard! forrard! my little darlings," as he saw them flying ahead, and forgot everything else, except that he was with them. What mattered it to him so long as Joe got safely over after him who else followed? How some got in, how others, led by the parson, made for the nearest bridge or ford, hoping to cut in again. Hounds were running, scent breast high, and he was with them! On they went to a small covert, where they might have changed had not Joe been back to view her double. A light lift helped them, and they got on good terms, back again some way, then turned short to the right, on to Highfirs Common, where she puzzled them some time amongst the furze, and allowed the field to come up. They had been running about thirty minutes pretty straight, but it was nearly over. How pleased the field were to get to them, and what a run it had been! The boy on the dun cob had a lot to say about his doings, but his sister quietly snubbed him, "How about the brook?" This seemed to get his monkey up, for when hounds drove their hare out on to the racecourse and went straight along, every one in view at racing pace, he rode his cob in front as hard as he could go. Off the racecourse into a small spinney, where the hare doubled, there was a high stile, over which the Master popped on his grey to pick up his hare in case they killed her. With more pluck than judgment the boy went too fast; game as a pebble, the dun tried his best, but had too much pace to rise, and as the Master picked up his hare stiff and stark for a "Whoo-whoop!" the pony hit the stile hard, and fell. Luckily the pace was such that the boy was shot clear, rolling like a cannon-ball yards ahead on the soft ground.

Loud laughed the Master, who was taken to task by an old gentleman for his heartlessness. "Bless your kind soul, sir, if you had seen and had as many falls as I have you would know when a man is hurt or not! Here, boy, come here and take the scut, for you have earned it well, and will make a sportsman some day. Take my advice, and always go slow at timber."

The boy looked pleased, though a bit shaken, as he came to take the scut, but soon mounted his pony again, none the worse but more sobered, as he rode off home with his sister.

"Who are they?" said the Master, as he mounted his chestnut to look for another hare.

"They belongs to the lady as has taken old Mr. Jones's cottage down at Heathfield," said Joe, who had managed to make inquiries as they rode along. "She's a widdy, with them two childer."

"Not a bad-looking lass, and rides well," soliloquised the Master, as he rode along. "How she came at the brook, and it takes some doing too. I wouldn't let a she relation of mine hunt, though, blest if I would."

"Hoick! holloa! Yonder she goes." And they were away once more, racing like the wind. The chestnut was young, and wanted riding; so he was soon engrossed with the business in hand; and a rattling fall over some stiff rails, which the young one would go at too fast, put everything else out of his head until he had killed another hare and arrived at home, after a capital day's sport, and sitting down in his old tweed suit to his dinner he began to think about the fair girl he had seen that day.

Before going further, a few words about the tenant at Heathfield will be necessary. Mrs. Scott was the widow of a well-to-do City merchant, who had left her well off, with her daughter Mary and son Tom, whom we have seen out with the hounds to-day. Having a comfortable house in town it was her custom to let it every now and then for a term, and take a cottage in the country for change of air— sometimes for six months and even for a year, or perhaps two, if they liked the neighbourhood. Thus they came to be living in Mr. Jones's cottage at Heathfield. Rose Cottage it was called, and a snug little place it was, nestling in a quiet corner of the village, well guarded by a thick hedge and sheltered with high trees. Roses bloomed nearly all the year round, and everything in the garden was earlier in the season than elsewhere. In the stables were a useful brougham horse, which carried the staid coachman in attendance behind his young mistress when wanted, the bay mare and dun cob before mentioned, which also ran in a pony-chaise to draw mother and daughter about when they did not care to have the brougham.

Mrs. Scott was one of those kind, well-meaning ladies who try to do right, but are too easily led; moreover, she was a little ambitious, like all mothers, that her only daughter should do well for herself in the matrimonial market.

Sitting reading in the pretty little drawing-room, she kept looking with anxious eye through the French window, commanding a view of the carriage drive, and just before two o'clock her face lighted up as she caught sight of her young people returning from their ride; Tom, in advance, waving his trophy in high glee, forgetting, boy-like, all about his dirty coat, which caught his fond mother's quick eye at once. Quickly opening the window she stepped out. "Oh,

Tom, what is the matter? you have had a fall. And Mary, your mare is all covered with dirt. What have you been doing, and what makes you so late? I have waited luncheon this hour for you."

Tom had first say, of course. "We have had a rare lark, mother, with the harriers, and the huntsman has given me this; I shall go out with the fox-hounds and get a brush like Cousin Fred next, then he won't be able to crow so next half. Dun Brown tumbled down, but we are not hurt, and I don't care a bit."

"We met the harriers, mother dear; don't look so anxious; it is better fun than always riding about these dull lanes; and you know Uncle William told us Mayfly had been hunted and was quiet with hounds when he bought her for us at Tattersall's, and we only had a little gallop with them," said Mary, quietly ignoring her performance at the brook and hoping that no one would tell mamma.

"I don't like your hunting," said Mrs. Scott. "If Tom likes to go out now and then with old George to look after him, I do not mind; but for you, Mary, it is too fast, and I don't like young ladies to go scampering about the country, it gets talked about."

"I don't see any harm in it, mother, and I am sure lots of girls hunt regularly, and are none the worse for it. The harriers that we met are a private pack, belonging to Mr. Hardacre, who hunts them himself, and seems a very nice young gentleman," said Mary, who knew a good deal more about the whole establishment of the Master of Harriers than any one would have guessed.

She was a tall, fair girl, that no one would have passed, even in a big crowd, without looking at her twice. A handsome rather than a pretty face, for there was at times a hard, determined expression about the mouth and lower features that gave one the idea of a temper. She possessed a beautiful figure, especially on horseback, when set off by a neat habit, and she sat her horse to perfection.

Though only nineteen years of age, she had completely gained the upper hand over her devoted mother, who was careful never to thwart her.

Tom, fourteen years old, was a fair specimen of the average schoolboy. Frank, open, and manly, better at sport than lessons, perhaps; but a boy is none the worse for that, so long as he goes straight.

He loved his dun pony like his own soul, and after seeing him washed over and done up, to be sure that no harm had been done by his fall, he had to feed his terriers and ferrets before going in to luncheon.

With a couple of well-bred fox-terriers, Grip and Nell, and three or four ferrets, he would trot about from farm to farm during his holidays, begging a day's ratting, or even rabbiting when in luck, and farmers were generally glad to see the boy, for he was a nailer at that game.

By the time he went in to luncheon, of course he forgot to wash his hands, so he had to be despatched forthwith, and on his return he found Mary had changed her habit, and with her mother was more than half through luncheon.

There was a quiet, determined look on the young lady's face as she said, "You leave me alone, mother. I know how to play my cards, and will not allow your foolish fears to spoil my game."

With a distressed look, the mother turned to Tom. "Well, Tom, as your sister wants to hunt, you must go with her, and I shall send George with you as well, for it does not look well for you two to be tearing about together alone."

"All right, mother, old George (won't get far on the brougham horse with those hounds, he was going to say, but a kick under the table from Mary stopped him, and he altered) likes hunting and knows a lot about it, and you know both ours are safe to jump anything that the brougham horse will." So it was settled that the young people might join the hounds whenever they were able.

Never was such a season known for sport in the annals of the Ravensdale Hunt. Day after day they had clipping runs, and as his young hounds had entered well, while of course they improved daily, the pack did not require quite such close attention on the Master's part as they might have done, so he found himself often watching for the flutter of a habit instead of being engrossed with his hounds as before; while at night, instead of thinking over the events of the day with his quiet pipe and grog after dinner, "How Bonnybell had made a hit in a stony lane," or "how beautifully the little darlings puzzled out a cold scent on stained ground," it was more often, "How well the girl rides. What a nice figure on horseback. She seems kind, too!" For they were already on bowing terms, and would say a few nothings out in the field, while he and Master Tom had struck up a strong friendship. John Hardacre, farming his own land— six hundred acres—with a good balance at his bankers, might have taken a very good position in the county, and mixed in the highest society; but he preferred a quiet life, as his father had done before him, and though he could entertain a duke at Ravensdale, or would meet at a nobleman's house with the harriers at any time, he had never availed himself further, though it was not for the want of asking. He had never been much in ladies' society, so was shy and reserved, while his usual good-humoured smile and ready wit seemed to disappear in their presence. Amongst men he was the life and soul of any company in which he might find himself. There was a perplexed look on his face now that was most comical as he sat before the fire, a strong black briar-root pipe between his white teeth, a glass of hot gin-and-water on his knee, and a favourite old harrier bitch, whose day was done, stretched out between his feet, starting in her dreams now and then at the recollection of many a merry chase in happy days gone by.

His banker's book lay open on the table beside him, and from time to time, after a sip, he would turn to it and seem to make calculations. " What would it cost ? She seems a nice, quiet, domesticated girl, fond of riding. Of course, I should not let her hunt though ; for women, especially married ones whose husbands are otherwise occupied, have no business out with hounds. She might ride about, though, as much as she likes, and have the choice of the nags into the bargain. What a lot it would put on their price at Tattersall's ; ' lots 1 to 8 carry a lady,' in the catalogue, after what I have to say for them, would quite cover the extra expense. But then she won't look at the like of me ! What do I know except hunting ? Dear old governor, he meant well, and so far I never grumbled, for no man has enjoyed life better, but he handicapped me heavily against the young men in my position of the present day when he neglected my education. A good many of them look down upon me, I know, though they are glad enough to come out with the hounds. But dash it all, old man, you are getting down-hearted ; why should you fret about other people ? " continued he to himself. " Can't I spreadeagle a field ? ' Faint heart never won fair lady.' There will be no harm in calling, and it is only neighbourly, anyhow. Old Jones used to walk a puppy, perhaps they might ; the boy is a trump, anyhow. I will go there the first frosty day that we can't hunt." Having made up his mind, he finished his glass and betook himself to bed at half-past ten.

The opportunity arrived before he expected. The hounds often met at Heathfield village, and during the first week in December they were there on a good scenting day. A small field met the Master as he rode up to the village green, where they always met. Among them, of course, were Miss Scott and her brother. Off came the Master's cap as the young lady rode up, and very gracious was her bow in return, while Master Tom rode right in amongst the hounds to invite John to Rose Cottage if he required refreshment.

Though contrary to his usual custom, he made a move in that direction, much to the delight of the young people and astonishment of the field. It is not every small house that will stand a siege at a moment's notice, but Mrs. Scott was quite equal to the occasion, and after our Master had been presented, and his wants and those of his men been attended, she received his stammering thanks and apologies so graciously, being in reality prepossessed by his good looks and modest demeanour, that when he turned his horse and left with the hounds to make room for the rest of the field, who were waiting to be attended—for a lot of hunting men are like a flock of sheep, if one rides up to a house to drink another does whether he wants it or not—he felt quite at home, and not a bit shy, when Mary ranged her bay mare alongside his horse to ride down the carriage drive.

Joe stared at his Master in open wonder, for there was the bay mare right amongst the hounds, and he who was usually so particular was actually talking and laughing with her fair rider regardless that his pets were in danger of being kicked.

Mary was gradually helping him out of his shyness, and all that day she rode beside him, and on many a day after that, till just before Christmas a hard frost set in, and all field operations were brought to a standstill.

John in a frost, with his occupation gone, was always uncomfortable, but now he seemed worse than ever.

For the first three or four days he went about his daily duties as usual, looking to his farm and exercising his hounds, but his nights grew duller and duller, so at last he could stand it no longer, and once his mind was made up it took a good deal to turn him.

He got himself up rather more carefully than usual, though always very neat in his sporting *mufti*, and having old Jack-of-all-trades roughed, he rode over to call at Rose Cottage.

Though a bright frosty morning, with keen wind, which seemed to cut through and freeze his very marrow, for he dared not go fast on the hard ground to keep warm, yet he felt himself grow hotter and hotter, until he would have been at white-heat on arrival, but just as he turned the corner from a narrow lane into a foot-path, for of course he knew every short cut, he came all of a sudden face to face with Mary Scott, looking better than ever, with the bloom of health from her enjoyment of sharp exercise. He was down from his cob at once, and the greeting was most cordial on both sides.

Mary asked how he managed to employ himself this weather, how were the hounds, naming one or two favourites, a sure way to win a huntsman's heart. John was enraptured, but when she led him on to talk about the horses, and let out that the bay mare was lame, he was so distressed that he blurted out—

"Well, never mind, you shall have one of mine when the frost goes. I wish you would take your choice, and as for that, look here, Miss Scott. May I call you Mary? I'm a rough, plain fellow, I know, but have a good heart somewhere."

Encouraged by her blushing, he seized her, covering the pretty face with kisses; nor did he leave go until she had promised to be his wife, subject to asking mamma; while old Jack-of-all-trades looked on demurely, a quiet spectator. If horses could only talk, what rum tales they could tell! But no one should reveal secrets concerning the old, old story; so, suffice it to say, it was arranged between the young people that John should go on to Rose Cottage with his important mission, while Mary continued her walk, to return home later on to hear the verdict.

However John got through that interview with the mother no one ever knew, but she helped him most kindly, and almost put him at his ease, though he confided to a friend afterwards that he would sooner go at the biggest fence possible, on the worst brute ever mounted, than face such an ordeal again.

However, he came through all right, and the old lady seemed well satisfied with his answers to her somewhat pertinent question as to his means. So she congratulated Mary when she came in, and as Tom was in great form when he heard the news, they all sat down to luncheon in good spirits.

It was quite a new experience for John to be treated as a member of a family; but he seemed to fall into their ways unconsciously, and after passing a very lively afternoon, helping Tom do some rat-hunting, with Mary looking on, till it grew dark, and sitting in a cosy room, with only the firelight, afterwards till dinner time, for the first time in his life he forgot all about his hounds and horses.

Weather mattered little, he seemed to be in perpetual sunshine. Taking no heed of the time, it was very late when old Jack was brought round, and after an affectionate leave-taking (it is a question whether John had ever been kissed before), he started on his homeward ride, and, as was his wont when highly pleased, began talking to his horse.

"Forrad on, old man! You will have this journey often enough now, I hope. She's a darling, isn't she? And she kissed you, too. I love her even better for being fond of animals. You shall carry her one day if you behave. Won't you be proud? But she shall have her pick of the stud, though she might do worse, eh, old horse? You won't be jealous?" It did not take them long to reach home; but it was nearly one o'clock, and the establishment were all sitting up anxiously waiting for their Master, and wondering what had kept him so unusually late. The news was too good to keep, and all were glad to hear it, for they loved their Master and were glad to hear anything that gave him pleasure. Talking it over next day amongst themselves, when the Master had again ridden over to dine at Rose Cottage, old John, who was a pretty keen judge of character amongst the human race as well as in the kennel, said, "She's a handsome girl, and well shaped; sits her horse well with good hands, but she never looks you straight in the face. Love hides a lot of faults, but you never knew the Master, or his father before him, keep a hound that did not look straight. I like to see an eye meet mine without fear, and look straight at me. See old Sempstress there, how confiding she looks at you, and she never told a lie."

"Well, grandfather, it's no good croaking, let's hope the Master will keep her straight; he's a rare good sort, and there is not a man can ride with him on this side of the country," said young John. "Here's luck to him, and long life," emptying a horn of ale that had been sent out for them.

Much to our Master's regret, he heard on arrival at Rose Cottage that the Scotts had accepted an invitation to spend Christmas in London with a Mr. Wright, who had married a sister of Mrs. Scott's, and John was now asked to join them and be introduced to their family. As the frost looked like lasting he accepted, and they were all to travel together two days before Christmas. He did not feel like himself leaving home at Christmas for the first time in his life, but he left the wherewithal for his people to enjoy themselves, and instructions to Joe where to telegraph in case of a thaw. The hounds and horses were quite safe. He knew well enough he could depend on his men, though he had seldom left them before. They had a merry journey to London, but after our Master had gone through the ordeal of introduction it must be confessed he felt like a fish out of water. Town with him meant Tattersall's, where he always resorted through the summer or during a frost; but he hated London, and never went anywhere but what he called the "boots and breeches" end of Oxford-street to give orders to Bartley or Tautz. Everything else he bought in his own village or the county-town, saying that it is the duty of every hunting man to spend money in his own neighbourhood amongst the people who support him. Christmas morning was dull, foggy, and miserable, very different to what he had been used, for even during a frost it is not quite so dismal out in the country. It looked like a thaw, which rather raised his spirits; but no telegram came from Joe. Mr. Wright was a City man, and knew nothing about sport. Even his attempts at that kind of conversation would have amused John at any other time, but now he seemed ill at ease. There were no sporting papers of course in the middle of the week, and nowhere to go. Mary, too, seemed cooler, for her town-bred cousins had been criticising her lover's countrified dress and manners, and she was rather inclined to snub him. Tom kept them all alive with his good spirits, and taking John out for a walk in the afternoon, they found their way down to old Tom Wilton's, at Notting-dale, and spent an hour amongst the hounds, chaffing and laughing, which put John quite in a good humour again, so he could even put up with Mr. Wright after dinner, and when they joined the ladies our Master was in great form. Next morning a welcome telegram arrived from Joe, and by the afternoon he was whirling along home in an Express. A capital day's sport next day, and his lady-love being still away, gave him the opportunity of writing his first love-letter, and a droll production it was. It is only under exceptional circumstances that such letters are ever produced in public, so it will not do to give it; suffice it to say it was duly answered, and that answer, together with a photograph of its sender, were deposited in our Master's breast-pocket, to be studied and gazed at times without number. There were a good many letters passed between them after that, for the Scotts remained in town, and as the weather continued open, John was fully occupied, and good sport kept him at home.

His season ended the last week in March, but the fox-hounds went on later, so he would go five days a week with them. The Scotts came down just before Easter, so John trotted over on Good Friday.

The fox-hounds were to meet near Heathfield next morning, and Mary wished to go. Her mare was not fit, of course, and Tom was not at home to go with her, so what could John do but offer to take her, though he hated to see ladies out hunting, and especially feared to take the one he loved, for no one knew better the risk that all run with hounds? With men it don't matter whether they fall or not, they can get clear; but a lady is so dependent on her horse, and if he falls she cannot often get away.

Miss Mary pouted so prettily, and showed just a little temper, that he was obliged to give way on the condition that she rode his grey, a very safe mount, and that she should go home with Joe, who would look after her when his Master changed horses.

It was a lovely morning, and they had a pleasant ride to the meet, one of the prettiest spots in the county. An old-established pack were the Blazershire, and it took a good man and horse to follow them over their grass country when the fences were made up. The huntsman, a tough, wiry little man, greeted John cordially as he rode up, for they were on the best of terms, and always helped one another in every way, as all good sportsmen should, when hunting different game over the same country.

John's engagement was pretty well known, and every one was gratifying his or her curiosity by staring at the young lady, who seemed quite composed under the ordeal. It was too bad of the M.F.H., who was a wag in his way, to pretend to ignore her presence, and without waiting for John to make the necessary introduction, launch out in a torrent of chaff, and tell a racy tale as in days gone by, enjoying his victim's discomfiture. Poor John had a bad quarter of an hour, as our lively neighbours over the water put it, and he was not sorry when the signal was given to move.

The first cover was a sure find, and answered its reputation now. Tally-ho!—Away! the pack streamed out of cover, and the rush began.

"Come along, Mary, let's keep out of the crowd. Keep close to the missis, Joe, in case we get parted." For it was too near the end of the season for a keen man to lose a run for any one, however dear.

"Yonder he goes, look! We can get over here and nick in with them. Sit well back, but it's no use telling you how to ride." A few small fences to a farm, where the fox was headed and turned back right through his pursuers, making his way to where he was first found. There he met with some late comers, so had little chance with the Blazershire bitches close to him.

"Whoo-whoop! tear 'im and eat 'im!" Almost a chop, they would hardly have saved his brush, had not John begged it and presented it to Mary, fastening it to the bridle and sending her home quite content with Joe. They had a good run in the afternoon, taking them right away from home, so it was late when John called at Rose Cottage on the way home, and his horse being tired he could not stop.

It was the end of the season, and in past years John had felt regret, but now he did not seem to mind a bit, for he had plenty to occupy him.

They were to be married in July, and he had to get his house done up and re-furnished. Much of his time was spent with Mary, and they had many pleasant rides together about the pretty country lanes. All went happily till nearly the end of May. The Wrights came down to stay at Rose Cottage. Mr. Wright, who was what is called a man of business, managed all Mrs. Scott's affairs, and he took in hand the task of settlements for Mary. Straightforward and honest as the day, John had no objection to his books being overhauled, but Mr. Wright being a Cockney could not

"WHO-WHOOP! TEAR IT UP!"

understand some of the expenditure. "Why should a man spend nearly a thousand a year on a pack of hounds?" he asked Mrs. Scott, and impressed on that good lady that the harriers ought to be given up. The Miss Wrights, too, used their influence on Mary, wondering how a good-looking girl like her should throw herself away on a man who dressed like an ostler (mark their ignorance), and had no ideas beyond hunting. They would do better, or leave it alone. Mary had not much real strength of character with all her obstinacy, so after the first excitement of her engagement wore off she began to slight poor John, and now she was even cruel. His love never changed, and he felt it keenly, for when he rode over to Rose Cottage now he knew that he was slighted. Mary snubbed him more than ever, and while the Wright girls were with her she seemed to take a delight in doing so. Mrs. Scott threw out strong hints that he ought to give up the hounds, but he never believed in anything of the sort, so took no notice till Mary one day put it to him rather strongly that he thought more of his hounds than he did of her.

This opened his eyes, but he did not say much till Mr. Wright made it one of the conditions that they should be given up before his niece was married, as the estate did not, in his eyes, justify the expenditure. Then our Master grappled with the situation.

Cantering over to Rose Cottage he found Mary alone in the garden, and asked her straight out whether it was by her desire that her uncle had made the proposition.

He looked so handsome in his anxiety and earnestness that she almost relented, but, determined to try him to the utmost, answered, "Yes."

"I am to understand that you will not marry me unless I give up my hounds?"

And she unfortunately again answered, "Yes."

"Then good-bye, Mary; I hope for your sake you will find some one more able to make you happy than I could."

And without trusting himself to say more, he galloped off home. Going at once to the kennels he shut himself in with his pets and gave vent to his feelings. They clustered round him in their affectionate, confiding way, poking their cold noses into his hand, and waving their sterns, while one or two old favourites took further liberties on this occasion, and jumped against him, looking up in his face, which brought him to himself.

"What love can ever equal yours, you beauties? Give you up! No, not for all the girls in England, nor marry at all unless they take you too. Yoick, Bonnybell, old bitch, look ye here, here's a photograph. Who-whoop! tear it up, there's an end to that game."

But for all this our Master felt his disappointment keenly, for a sportsman's affections are not lightly given. An old friend met him in the county town a short time after with a furnishing catalogue under his arm, going to the leading upholsterers. He had heard of his engagement without hearing the later news, and not having had the opportunity before of congratulating him on the first event, proceeded to do so in the usual gushing manner. There was a quiet twinkle in the Master's eye as he said, "There were a good many kind friends offered their congratulations before, but you are the first this time, and really I think there is more cause to thank you than all the others put together, for it would be no use for me to marry a girl who objected to a pack of hounds."

"My dear fellow, I am very sorry, but no apology on my part will do for a mistake that I could not help, and you are a good sort. Come and have a drink."

"Well, I don't often indulge between meals, as you know, but my appetite has not been very good lately, and I don't feel quite up to the mark."

Any one could see that his usually hard bitten face was marked with lines, and he had evidently suffered more than he would have cared to show.

"What are you doing with that catalogue, if it is a fair question?" said his friend.

"Well, you know I had given orders for my house to be done up, and when I give an order or put a horse at a fence it has to be done, whatever happens. Going through life is very like a run with hounds; there are difficulties and fences to be encountered, and now and then the best of us come to grief. A shake like I have had is like a bad fall, which turns us back on the wrong side of a fence. If we can't get over we go round, and next time we come to the same kind of fence, usually a darned blind one, we go steady, gather him well together, and pick out the easiest place."

As his friend said good-bye, and stood watching his well-knit active figure as he walked down the street with that slight rolling gait peculiar to men who are always in the saddle, he could not help wishing that "the next time our friend John meets with a fence of this description that he will get safe over, for his sort is getting precious scarce."

When the hare-hunting season commenced again there was no change in the Ravensdale pack, but a very neat little pony-chaise might have been seen at the opening meet, driven by pretty little Fanny Brown, daughter of one of the largest tenant farmers in the county, and there were rumours about that all that new furniture at Ravensdale had not been bought for nothing.

A board, "To Let," stood in the garden of Rose Cottage. Poor Tom never got over the disappointment, for he felt it more than any one, and there was no hunting to be had in London, where they had gone.

After an engagement has been made public, and a girl breaks it off, it makes other men careful. Some one saw Mary walking in town with a young man whose character, they said, would not bear very strict investigation, for all that he wore a black coat and a high hat. But if she liked to console herself for what even she now reckoned her loss, it was no one else's business. It will not be out of place to give a word of advice to well-meaning but meddlesome persons. If a sportsman gives his love it is not done without due consideration and knowing what he can afford best, so never interfere with the Ruling Passion.

THE RULING PASSION—SEQUEL.

THE RULING PASSION—SEQUEL.

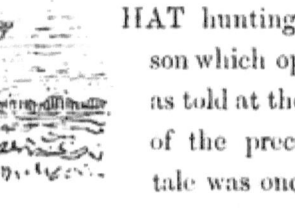

HAT hunting season which opened as told at the end of the preceding tale was one tha will never be forgotten by worthy John Hardacre or his followers, who still declare it to be the best, as it was also the last that they ever enjoyed with the Ravensdale Harriers. On the opening day there was a neat little pony-chaise driven by pretty little Fanny Brown, and rumour with busy tongues declared that the Master was sorely smitten by her charms, but once bit twice shy, he was not struck all of a heap, for past experience made him wary, besides which his hounds now occupied his whole attention, for never before had they shown such sport; so the ruling passion was stronger than ever. Not that he was altogether insensible to the fair Fanny's charms, for she had many fascinating ways which were almost soothing to his feelings still smarting under previous wounds, but she was young yet, and if ever he thought much about her it was with the reflection that she was not more than eighteen, so her parents would not be likely to favour any suitor for some years, especially as she would inherit a goodly dowry, about fifty thousand pounds, if she married according to their satisfaction. Perhaps his natural modesty stood in his way, and the ruling passion still more, for old Brown was one of his supporters with greater influence than most of them, so he naturally argued to himself that if he did anything to upset their hitherto friendly relations, it might possibly alter hunting arrangements. So he kept on hunting and showing rare sport, which made his little pack more popular than ever. His horses carried him better and he rode harder than ever, so being wrapt up in sport heart and soul he never noticed anything else.

Poor Fanny Brown! She was a nice little girl, but had unluckily imbibed romantic notions at a dangerous age and fancied that every man must fall in love with her, which, however harmless such fancy may be to girls less favourably dowered, was a source of danger to her, rendering her liable to become the prey of unscrupulous fortune-seekers,—but of this anon.

Her pony-carriage was often seen out with the harriers near old Brown's farm, which was about twelve miles from their kennels.

John always had a joke or kind word ready for children, and especially those belonging to his supporters, nor did he notice as he grew older that they were doing the same; so he treated them all alike, big or little, with that good-natured simplicity that is most easily imposed upon by the precocious and unscrupulous youth of both sexes. He loved to see youngsters in the saddle, for he argued that if they were only properly entered they would grow up to carry on the best of all sports as their elders drop off. Old Brown having only one child, John had always been perhaps more attentive to her than if she had been one amongst six. He had been the first to put her on horseback while he was still a lad whipping-in to his father's hounds, and she but a toddling child in pinafores, twelve years ago, and he still treated her almost as a child, till one day when his hounds met at her father's house during his engagement with Mary Scott the manner in which little Fanny Brown offered her congratulations would have set any one else thinking, but poor John was, luckily for his peace of mind, so ignorant of the ins and outs of love and life that he accepted all in faith, and, if the truth were known, so long as his hounds showed good sport on that particular day it mattered little to him whether congratulations on a love affair were genuine or not if scent served his darlings to get blood, and this season again they were showing such sport that he thought of nothing else.

In vain did Fanny don her best habit and ride old Patent Safety, one of her father's favourite hunters, as he had rarely been ridden before; often she was alone in the same field with the Master and Joe Wilson, who, remembering the fate of the other girl, would smile quietly as he turned hounds when necessary—for if they were at fault Master and man worked so well together that only the cleverest would ever see that hounds had ever thrown up. When once a man who has to do with hounds, either as huntsman or whipper-in, begins to take notice of outside matters it is all up with sport, and the sooner he is drafted the better. It is only the most ignorant amongst the field that expect those connected with hounds to pay attention to anything but their darlings when at work. So poor little Fanny relaxed her efforts, though it was with some reluctance, for he was quite a hero during this season, and his name was in everybody's mouth all over the country. During that year the Hares' and Rabbits' Bill had passed, so fur soon became so scarce, excepting in strictly preserved ground, where they were too thick for sport, that it was almost hopeless to go out hare-hunting; but John was equal to the occasion, for sooner than part with his darlings he procured some red deer and a deer-cart which made him quite independent.

Their first attempt at stag-hunting was not very successful, for the little hounds did not understand being cheered to hunt such big game, and still more were they astonished when they ran up to a great animal that knocked them about while he stood at bay, but after two or three days they were well blooded and soon ran so well that even their former season was eclipsed and their Master with his men in scarlet coats were more popular even than when they wore green. It was harder work, for they had longer distances to travel. Often a deer took them twenty or thirty miles from home, and John found his evenings at home shorter than ever.

Fanny Brown did not care much for stag-hunting, hounds went too fast and too far, and though the Master seemed pleased enough to have her company during a long ride home he would only jog along at that easy hounds' pace which is so tiresome to those unused to it. In vain did she try to force the pace, he only let her go on and jogged along quite contentedly with his darlings as usual, so she gave up all hope of captivating him, and soon rumours flew about that she was engaged to be married to a fast young man, who had come down from London with a small stud of hunters to stay in the village near old Brown's farm. When John heard of it he was sorry, for he really liked the little girl and by all accounts her choice was not a wise one, which her parents soon found out and set their faces against it. But Fanny was a very self-willed young lady, and even their threat of disinheritance did not prevent her from getting involved in a regular engagement. John saw her no more out hunting, but that troubled him not, for sport was so good that he had time for nothing else, and he finished the season with a great run that was the talk of the county through the summer.

When his horses went to Tattersall's that year they made more money than ever, and he had such a balance at his banker's that he determined to improve his pack and perhaps hunt next season three days a week instead of two. He soon bought a lot of good young horses and a few couples of small staghounds from the best kennels, besides the puppies that came in from walks, so he had forty couples in kennel. In June there was the usual race-meeting on the county course, and some of the young bachelors proposed a fancy-dress ball in the Town Hall the same night, so John was named as a steward and pledged to attend. He hated dancing though Mary Scott had taken great pains to teach him, but he could make himself useful as a steward and look after the card and oyster rooms which he stipulated should be set apart for those who, like himself, did not care for dancing. He was not one to give himself much trouble or go to any unnecessary expense for dress, but a new coat would be necessary for next season, so he appeared in a brand-new scarlet, and as he did not intend to dance he put on breeches, boots and spurs (without rowels), with even a new cap and whip in case any one wanted it, for as he said a steward is bound to keep order, and should be well prepared.

The race-meeting passed off well on a glorious June day, and most of the stewards, who had ridden long distances and been on horseback all day, dined together at the principal hotel in the evening. After a good dinner and a quiet smoke John enjoyed a cold tub before dressing for the ball, so when he put on his easy-fitting hunting clothes, to which he was most accustomed, and always liked best, for they reminded him of his happiest hours, he felt fit as a fiddle and ready for anything. If the truth were told he hardly knew himself as he sauntered—almost swaggered—into the ball-room, where many varied figures had begun to collect, but he saw no one that he knew as yet, so his courage gradually oozed out at his fingers ends, and even found its way down to the toes of Bartley's masterpieces—which he could not help confessing he would sooner put home in his stirrups and go at the biggest, blackest uncertainty in the shape of a rasper, than foot it in a dance with even the shyest *débutante* on these boards.

Just as he was looking out for a friend or a bolt hole, a white-gloved hand gently touched his arm and a familiar, soft voice asked, "Why look so cross? no one is riding over your hounds." And he started almost guiltily on recognising little Fanny, for did not she now belong nominally, if not morally, to another, so whatever he might feel himself she was none of his. So he answered coolly but kindly "Hulloa, little one, how are you? Am I looking cross? Your smiling face will soon cure that. How are your father and mother? I intend coming over to fetch my puppy at walk, and ask

"YOU ARE IN TROUBLE, LITTLE LADY?"

them to take another. You will look after it while you are at home, but I suppose we shall lose you soon if all is true?"

There was a quiver on her lip and tear in her eye as she was going to turn away. A man who hunts hounds is quicker in noticing trifles, and makes up his mind sooner than ordinary folks, so John saw at once that she was in trouble and it flashed through him, "poor little girl, she has no brothers, and having offended her parents has no one to go to for sympathy. I'm an old hulk thrown on one side, but might be useful, so here goes."

"You are in trouble, little lady, come and sit down in this corner and tell me all about it."

She looked up, smiling very roguishly through her tears, for she had many varying humours, "No! we must have a dance first or people might talk about us."

"I dance?" said John, "why I put on these boots so that no one should expect me to go careering about."

"Well, we must," said she; "come along, I will show you how."

It is bad enough to run across a ploughed field after a runaway horse, while all around looks starry from the effects of a cropper, but to run about even on slippery boards, which are comparatively easy going, for pleasure, a very little goes a long way, so our Master soon tired and did not feel quite himself again till he had absorbed about a pint of champagne-cup, while Fanny took an ice in the refreshment-room. Then they found a secluded corner while more energetic couples sorted themselves out for the next dance. John's ears were pretty quick as his eyes were sharp, and as he sat down to listen to Fanny's tale he overheard a young couple passing remark:

"He is soon off with the old love and on with a new!"

"Yes," said the other, "and she is on with a new without being off with the old."

Luckily Fanny did not hear these remarks or she could not have told her troubles, which would have saved John some though this little tale might never have been written.

During three consecutive dances, while others whirled round, refreshed themselves and changed partners, did that young couple sit in the same secluded spot. John forgot all about the whist-tables and even the oyster-room which had been placed under his superintendance, for he was sorely perplexed by the girl's troubles. Her father threatened to disinherit her, her mother was worse than furious, hardly ever speaking to her, while the young man had considerably cooled down from the ardour of first devotion, when he heard that her fortune was only conditional on a satisfactory marriage, and he was not the man so constituted.

Poor honest John, what could he do! After listening to the girl's tale with that quiet, sympathetic, almost caressing manner peculiar to sportsmen, that begets confidence amongst even the wildest or shyest of animals as well as human beings, he felt his heart unusually softened; and pity soon begets love, especially when he himself still felt just a little ill-used after his first love affair. He soon made up his mind how to help her, while they had another dance just before supper —to which he conducted her to a seat of honour at the stewards' table, which caused some talk amongst the company, by whom both were of course well known. After supper their flirtation continued, and they seemed so devoted to each other that Mrs. Brown hoped that all would yet be well with her daughter, who seemed to have forgotten even the existence of "that adventurer," as his would-be mother-in-law called him.

Fanny's fancy-dress was covered with gorgeous butterflies, so John begged one as a memento of the evening, and before handing her to their carriage he promised to ride over to call next day. That night, or rather morning, as he rode home from the ball on Jack-of-all-trades he began consulting his horse as usual. "What shall we do, old chap, when we get over to Hilsden Fields? Poor little girl, we must save her if possible, but how? Shall I propose to her myself and make her break off with that chap? If she likes to throw me over afterwards I shall be none the worse, for eels get used to skinning, and she may still care enough for me to make me a good wife, though I fear she is a bit too fast. Anyhow I shall be doing a good turn to old Brown, who has always been a rare good friend to me and a real sportsman too." Jack-of-all-trades did not say nay.

John was always an early riser, no matter what time he went to bed, which was seldom later than ten o'clock. This morning he had only two hours between the sheets, but refreshed by his tub, he was in the kennels soon after six. He walked out his darlings in the dew-sprinkled meadows and made a rare good breakfast before setting out on Jack-of-all-trades to ride twelve miles in the cool of the morning to Hilsden Fields. There he met Mr. Brown riding round his farm on a thick-set cob followed by the puppy at walk, so the two farmer-sportsmen were soon engrossed in congenial conversation till the flutter of a pink dress, as they neared the garden, reminded John that the object of his visit was not altogether connected with sport and agriculture. Perhaps John did not look so attractive in sober mufti as in scarlet, and this has some effect on young girls, but his reception by Miss Fanny was not half so cordial as he expected, and instead of offering himself as a sacrifice as he intended, he chatted quietly with Mr. and Mrs. Brown till it was time to return home. Then Fanny went out to see him mount, and as he was leaving said, " Are you going to ride at the horse-show here on Saturday ? "

" No," said he, " I have no horses fit to show, but I shall ride over to see it."

" Will you take me with you ? " said she, with a meaning look.

" Yes, with pleasure if you wish it."

Old Brown overheard this, and said, " You had better ride over early and stay here over Sunday." To which his daughter seemed to nod " yes." " So be it," said John as he rode away, little knowing that Fanny was even then negotiating to break off her first entanglement and that he was expected to help.

On Saturday while riding together to the horse-show, John noticed the girl change colour as a young man on foot stared hard at him with a wicked look in his eye that would have frightened one less bold, but he returned the stare with his keen brown eyes and saw how the other turned away from his penetrating look, so he knew that he had little to fear from that quarter. The horse-show and jumping performances passed off without any mishap, while John congratulated himself that he was there simply as a spectator instead of taking part in them as usual, while he amused his companion by commenting on the performers, most of whom were known to both of them. As they rode back to Hilsden Fields they were on very good terms with each other, and he asked her who was the young man that had looked at them so intently. The answer was as he expected, nor did she seem to care much about her intended. Next day after church they went for a long walk, and finding a quiet corner in one of Mr. Brown's coverts sat down for a talk.

Fanny admitted after some time that she did not care enough for her intended to thwart her parents' wishes. In fact he had been very disagreeable since he found that her fortune was dependent on them; but she did not see how she could break off, for he would not let her while a hope remained for him to secure her with her fortune. This was just what John expected, so he proposed himself on the condition that she should get her father's permission and break off the other engagement. He would give her time to consider and if she thought proper he would himself release her afterwards.

As he rode home next day, promising to come over again as soon as he heard from her, he thought it all over and confided in Jack-of-all-trades, knowing that no exaggerated tales would be started by the old horse.

"Well, we are in for it again, old horse, and may have a good many journeys over this way through the summer, but we must save that dear little girl if we can and you will not grumble." In two days time he received a letter from Fanny saying that she had broken off her first engagement and was only waiting to receive him when he had spoken to her father.

So Jack-of-all-trades jogged along once more, wondering what made his rider so unusually anxious. Why did those heels kick his ribs? and why were sentences of nsultation so short, instead of confidential? If horses really think and communicate with one another—there is no doubt but what they do—old Jack-of-all-trades must have been entertaining company to the inhabitants of old Brown's stables that day.

Fanny greeted John with great show of affection and told him that she was free till he asked her father's permission to claim her, so thus encouraged he went to his old friend and soon arranged matters to their mutual satisfaction, so once more John found himself bound for matrimony.

A twelve-mile trot on courting intent takes some doing, especially when a man has other occupations, so he was very glad when Fanny came to stay with an old aunt in the village near Ravensdale, where John could see her every day without trouble, and their time passed pleasantly, riding and driving about through the summer months. When she went back home John rode over to Hilsden Fields and learnt that she intended shortly leaving on a visit to the seaside. His puppy had been taken with distemper just as it should have been sent in from walk, so Mr. Brown kept it to nurse, for he liked to walk a good puppy and send it in so as to do credit to its walk. Fanny took a good deal of interest in this puppy and begged to have the care of it, so John was more than pleased.

"You must name it," said he one evening when it was walking out with them, "and I shall always think of you when I see her going to the front, for by her shape and make if she does not lead I shall be disappointed."

"I call her Agnostic," said Fanny.

"What a funny name, quite new in kennel books!" said John. "What does it mean?"

"It means a new religion," she said. "I am an Agnostic."

"Oh, if it is anything to do with you it must be divine," said he in good faith, "so I will enter her as Agnostic. I wonder what Joe will make of it, 'Huich to Agnostic,' 'Ware Oss Agnostic.' It will teach him to roll his tongue about." On his way home as he passed the foxhound kennels he met the Master, who was one of his best friends. "Hulloa, John," said the master of the foxhounds, "you seem to be often riding about on this side of the country. Courting again are you?"

"You know all about it," said John, "so stop chaff, and as you went to college perhaps you can tell me what an agnostic is. I have a hound called so."

The master of the foxhounds looked serious as he answered,

"Don't have anything to do with such a fraud. It means a thing that believes in nothing and never speaks the truth except by accident."

"Oh, lor!" said John as he rode home, "I'm in for more trouble, but I will bide my time and see how it turns out."

Fanny's aunt, who lived near Ravensdale, was one of John's admirers, and glad enough to get such a match for her niece, but when he went in to see her on the morning after this conversation and told her of it she looked grave, as any one who hears that others whom she loves are getting involved in unknown troubles, so she determined to talk seriously to Fanny at the first opportunity. Unluckily the young lady went away to the seaside while John was still busy at home, nor did the few letters that she wrote give him much encouragement to visit her, so he stayed at home, going through his ordinary routine of duty till August, nor did he make his usual tour to hunt on Exmoor that year, hoping and expecting day by day to hear that Fanny would return home, when he would be ready to receive her. Her letters were fewer and grew colder, while rumours reached Ravensdale that Fanny's first love was still pressing his claims in the hope that her parents might relent.

This riled John, for he looked upon himself as the protector of his old friend Brown's interests if not his own, so when Miss Fanny returned home he rode over the same day to bid her welcome, and was received so coldly that most lovers would have been disheartened.

On his way home he called on old Miss Brown and told her all. She shook her head and muttered something about "cross breeds, none such in our family before," ending up with, "Take care, John, you are a good man and worthy a better fate, but you will only get trouble in that quarter, though I say it of my brother's child."

Next morning came a letter from Fanny wishing to break off the engagement, so John trotted over to see Mr. Brown, and placed the whole matter in his hands. The old man's words were solemn. "As she makes her bed so must she lie on it. If she marries with my consent my fortune goes to her, but if not I can find other means to dispose of it. Have a talk to her, John, and hear what she has to say."

John talked long and earnestly, more perhaps like a father than a lover, but all to no purpose. The girl would not listen, and gave him such a decided answer that he rode home once more freed from care or tanglement. What were his feelings during his ride home? They soon took practical form for consolation. It was a soaking wet day after prolonged drought, so he stopped at the foxhound kennels to know if they would go out cub-hunting. The master of the foxhounds noticed nothing in John's appearance, for he showed no sign of disappointment or sorrow, and the master of the foxhounds was in high glee, for the rain gave him the chance to hunt and he would go out next morning at five o'clock. Would John ride over to help them? Would he not? for he felt that the sight of hounds hunting would do him good and his own could not begin for another fortnight yet, so he rode home and said nothing to anybody.

Next morning he was at the covert-side before five, and before hounds came a young farmer rode up with the news that Fanny Brown had eloped with her first love soon after John had left the previous afternoon. When the master of the foxhounds arrived he had no thought for anything but his hounds, nor did he notice John till they had killed a cub, that John had hulloaed away and ridden like a demon over the blindest fences where no one dared follow, so he held up the dead cub alone, and those who knew him best noticed a wild look about his eye, and lips drawn tight instead of his usual smile.

"Hulloa, John, what's the matter?" said the master of the foxhounds as he took the carcase from him to blood the young ones. John's answer did not convey all that he felt but was characteristic, showing that he wished to conceal his real feelings.

"Why I've lost fifty thousand pounds without doing good to any one. Who-whoop! blood your hounds, never mind about me!"

For a few days he was as savage as a bear, and nothing seemed to go right. His young hounds having had distemper so badly they were not judged at the puppy show till late in the summer, and the judges gave the prize to Agnostic, so he sent the cup over to Mr. Brown.

When they began hunting she gave a lot of trouble, always running riot, but he gave her every chance and at last thought that she would make a good hound. They had capital sport up to Christmas, when hard frost and snow set in, so they did not hunt for nearly a month.

Then they had some rare runs and no one enjoyed them better than the Master.

One day they had a very long run and scent failed suddenly with a beaten deer. Horses were tired and hounds hunted inch by inch. Twice Agnostic led them wrong, while the whips galloped their weary horses to put them right. The third time was in a covert, she threw her tongue and looked up in the Master's face so confidently that he gave her a cheer so the rest flew to head, only to throw up in disgust, and his quick eye pricked a hare instead of the slot of his deer. In a fit of justifiable passion he jumped off his horse, and hit Agnostic on the head with his hammer-headed whip, telling Joe to hang her on a keeper's tree that was handy. As he trotted off to make good his cast he said bitterly, "So should all liars be treated, and there would be less trouble in the world."

On their way home as they passed the wood Joe rode up alongside his Master,

"That butt end of yours, sir, has saved a lot of our whipcord. I was never so pleased to put a hound out of the way before, and it was quite right not to wait till we got home."

"Yes," said the Master, "I might have let her off as I have done so often on account of her good looks but I could not stand such a lie, and we should never have taken the deer, but you had better go and bury her. There is an old saw-pit close by which will do, then jog on after us."

That hunting season ended well as it began, and they finished with a great run from Hilsden Fields nearly to the sea, twenty miles off. Amongst the field were Mr. Brown, and a favourite niece, Nellie Brown (one of a large family), who had come to live with her uncle and aunt. The old gentleman did not get to the finish but she did with only three others besides the Master and his men. On their way home she accompanied them, a pleasant, quiet girl about twenty years of age, and it was a regular case of love at first sight. With John's horse tired, she insisted on giving him hers, while she jogged along, a much lighter weight, on his, so the whips, with their weary nags, were not near enough to disturb the conversation. Of course she knew all about John and how he had been treated by her cousin, wondering at the same time how Fanny could have been so foolish, not to say wicked. She would like to have the chance to marry such a man. John's thoughts too, as he jogged along amongst his darlings, were not altogether about them though he saw with pride that they trotted gaily along with sterns up as if setting out instead of returning from a severe run. Then he turned his clear eyes on his companion, noticing how lightly she played with her horse's mouth, just letting him feel that he had a rider on his back in case he needed assistance, for he was sadly tired. He saw too that she had a pretty figure, set off to best advantage by a well-fitting habit, and her fair hair was neatly braided under a low round hat, the perfection of neatness and simplicity. Then their eyes met, and though a soft blush rose to her face she did not avert her pretty blue eyes but returned his look with one of modest confidence.

"At last," thought John, "I have found true happiness," nor did he throw away the chance. Before they reached Hilsden Fields they were betrothed, and John did what he had never done before in his life. He sent his men home with the hounds and stayed the night with old Brown, who was really pleased to get John as a relation, so was old Miss Brown, on whom he called as he rode home next morning.

Old Brown was very liberal in the matter of marriage settlements and they were married early in June. The members and followers of the Ravensdale Staghounds presented their Master with a wedding present for which they subscribed £1,000. His men gave him a silver horn and hammer-headed whip of the same metal, both of which he carried on their opening day in November, when a large field met him at the kennels. Mrs. John Hardacre made a charming hostess, and seemed never happier than when furthering the interests of sport, and after her husband her chief pride was the Ravensdale pack.

SHALL I?

SHALL I?

WHAT an odd title for a tale!" most readers will remark; and if it was a book that had to be written, no doubt some explanation would be given in an elaborate preface why such was chosen, but in a short story it need only be said of these two simple words of interrogation "Shall I?" if any one gets into the habit of reflecting for the second or two while he repeats them to himself, he will keep out of a lot of trouble into which undue haste might precipitate others less cautious. Prudence does not mean deficiency of pluck, for how often quiet perseverance shows to the front when exuberant dash has dwindled away, and the steady interrogator "Shall I?" goes by him that has been all " I will."

"Poor old Tom," there he sat in a wagonnette with his wife and large small family behind him, on Monday, the 1st of November, 18—, when the Horsemanshire Hounds met at

Selby Gate for their opening day. There was a hunting look about the game old brown horse in the shafts, and well there might be, for was it not poor old Harkaway? the sole remnant of as good a stud of weight-carriers as ever welter crossed. A bandage on the near fore-leg told that it was not to be trusted, and thereby hangs a tale to be noted further on. There was a look of sorrow, perhaps, when the keen eye of his driver looked over the pack as they walked by, but that eye, practised as it was, could detect no fault either in hounds or horses, on which the servants of this crack pack were mounted; for he would follow them no more, and those who rode up to greet him noticed with sorrow that he had grown a beard, so they knew that his hunting days were over, for had he not always said that "Hunting was the only thing worth the trouble of shaving for," and now he had given it up. Poor old Tom! We had been at school and college together, both of us came into comfortable competences, and lived together for some years after like brothers, though not related. Till the day he married we were inseparable. In the winter we hunted from our snug little box in Horseman-shire, and no two men had more comfortable quarters or kept a better stud. We had six hunters each, and a joint-stock Qui-tamer that went in the brougham or dog-cart, hacked and carried us or our friends with hounds when wanted, doing about three times the work of any other, and always fit to go. Sometimes he lasted, and sometimes went to pieces, but never cost us much, for we used to pick up Qui-tamer out of the cheap lots at Tattersall's, robbing the cabbies of their legitimate prey, for no matter if Qui-tamer had a temper, or any little infirmity, he was bound to go, and so long as he had four good legs hard work kept him in order, for he had no time for mischief. In the summertime, when we summered our hunters at home, and bought elaborate hacks to ride in the Row, and Polo ponies for the game of which we were fond, Qui-tamer drew the brougham about at nights, and by way of rest at the end of the week towed our barge up and down the river as fancy moved us.

Those were merry days, and our life together was one round of pleasure; till one day Tom fell in love with, as he said, the jolliest girl in creation! He said this almost apologetically to such an old friend, for we had almost sworn to live and die together; but the day of reckoning must come some time, and though so far the self-interrogatory "Shall I?" had kept us out of many dilemmas, for every man falls in love naturally during the summer months, when there is nothing else to do, but the golden rule "Shall I?" just at the critical moment, when the fair syren had perhaps hooked us in a corner with mamma watching, had averted danger, till Tom succumbed. They had been spooning about together all through the hunting season, but it was a bright warm June day on the river that did the mischief, when we had been to a picnic on the barge, and, to his honour be it known, that Tom came at once to tell his old friend, but added insult to injury by recommending the same course at the first opportunity. Well it was to put a good face on it, and offer the first congratulations, as an old friend to the young lady, who certainly was a clipper, but it is dreadful to lose one like a brother, as is always the case by marriage, for he can never be the same after; though it was hard lines on Qui-tamer for wrath to be expended on him in showers of stones thrown from the bow to make him walk faster and get home, for he had done nothing wrong except mutely helping to tow those young people together.

Once he had made up his mind, never was mortal man in such a hurry to get married. The 1st of July was fixed, and he wanted so much assistance in the way of house-hunting and buying furniture, that we had a very busy time, and, needless to say, he did not bear the brunt of the hard work, for was not she wanting his attendance? So it was always, "I say, old fellow, you won't mind going down to look at such and such a house, just to see if it will do for us?" Luckily, a nice little house, with a few acres of grass-land round it, fell vacant in Horsemanshire, only about five miles from our snug hunting-box, so that was the very thing. It did not require much doing to it, so they could marry at once, go away on their honeymoon, and meanwhile it would relieve my sorrowful dulness to get the furniture in, and have it all comfortable for them on their return.

It was a merry wedding as weddings go, and of course Tom would not trust any one but his oldest friend to lead him to the altar, and hold his head if necessary. Tom's speech at the breakfast was much as usual on these occasions, for with all his good qualities he lacked originality, and kept to old lines. Of course he recommended all his friends to follow his example, but did not the fox do the same when he lost his brush? and Tom was rather disconcerted by a wink, for there was nothing especially attractive about the bridesmaids, and when it is said they were a level lot, that is all, so there was no temptation to reflect "Shall I?" on this occasion. However, as a great authority says, "Words were given to us to conceal our thoughts," so the best man had to follow in much the same strain, and no one could guess at the real state of his feelings, which were something like this "Shall I? No! wait a bit to see how Tom gets on, there is plenty of time yet, and after all it may not be very dull living alone; at all events it is worth trying." Tom's pleasant companionship would be a great loss, and there was no other friend amongst a large acquaintance to take his place in the hunting-box.

During his honeymoon he wrote several times, evidently in a state of the highest happiness, of course; wanting to know how everything was getting on at Dale Lodge, his new place, which was becoming quite an elysium for the young couple on their return. Had it not been for the occupation of arranging that house, goodness knows what would have become of me, for it was dull indeed at first without Tom His only instructions were to spare no expense in decorating and furnishing; get the stables in order, and move his stud in as soon as possible. The stables were all right after being painted, four boxes and four stalls, which just held Tom's six hunters and his wife's two, that her father gave her for a wedding present. They bought a wagonette with a movable cover, and shafts and pole for one or a pair, in which Tom proposed to drive his hunters when necessary, but they would more often use the dog-cart, with perhaps a tandem. Up till now we had always shared stable expenses equally, all except buying or selling hunters, but profit or loss in Qui-tamer was mutual, and one stud-groom looked after the lot. Tom had neither room nor work for a Qui-tamer, so magnanimously gave up his share, and Jem Perks, our stud-groom, a quaint dry file, who had lived with us for some years, and thoroughly understood his duties, elected to stay on at the hunting-box when we gave him his choice, for he said that was a certainty, whereas the other place was an uncertainty, and showed his sense as subsequent events proved. So Bob Short, our second groom, went to Dale Lodge and took charge of the stud with three helpers, while Jem Perks engaged others in their places, for he soon made good stablemen out of raw material, and was second to none in the art of conditioning hunters. Tom and his wife came home just before the hunting season commenced, and were delighted with their new abode. Never did a prouder or happier young couple set out to meet hounds on the opening day in November, and it was worth going any distance to see Tom, always the pink of perfection, on his favourite Harkaway, then six years old, able to hold their own with the best of us; but Tom's look of admiration at his wife, as she sat gracefully on her thoroughbred bay mare, set many of us envying his good fortune, and "Shall I?" when a shrill "Tally-ho-Away!" set blood coursing and thoughts flying in another direction, and for the next forty minutes our delight was concentrated in those dappled darlings, and our sole ambition to maintain pride of place. When the glad "who-whoop!" rang out clear and loud, Tom for once was not there to hear it. There had been no time for looking about even after nearest and dearest friends, but rumour said some mishap to Tom's wife was the cause; it must have been slight, for they came up before hounds moved away, and of course we said nothing. It was generally noticed that Tom was not in his old form, till just before Christmas Bob Short was seen on Harkaway at the meet, and it looked more like old times. "Holloa, Bob, master sent on?" "Yes, sir, he's riding one of the hacks, so

I shall have to go straight home. I never see hounds now, sir." This was said regretfully, for he was a good second horseman, and had seen a lot of hunting with Tom in former days. He was very fond of his good Master now, and was ready with his hunter to be mounted the moment he appeared on one of his wife's horses.

"Morning, Tom; missis not met with an accident, I hope?"

"Oh, no! she will drive to the meet to-morrow, but did not like the look of the weather this morning." Sure enough they appeared next day in the wagonette; Tom driving his wife's two hunters for exercise, as he said, and she seemed quite content to sit behind them.

There was a lot of frost that winter, and the long evenings were dull enough at home, and in catchy weather it did not do to be always running up to town, for that might lose a day's hunting, so Qui-tamer, shod with india-rubber, had plenty of running backwards and forwards between Dale Lodge, sometimes ridden, but more often driven, and in a sleigh, which was good fun when snow allowed its use, for he hated the bells, and could gallop like blazes when he bolted, which was a common occurrence. Tom was never allowed to risk his neck in the sleigh, so was quite dependent on my visits for amusement and getting all the outside news. Not that he ever grumbled or complained, but one who knew him so well could notice that he was not quite so cheery as formerly, and one day when he was alone in his study, having found out that Harkaway had a doubtful leg, since that time when he first rode him hard, he seemed downright cross, and was casting up his banker's book with quite an anxious face.

The hard winter kept everything backward, and prolonged the hunting season till nearly the end of April, but the best of all things must come to an end, and even on the grass it was getting hard and dry, when the Master sent out his cards for "Selby Gate," always the first and last day's meet, so we knew that the end had really come. Selby Gate was five miles beyond Dale Lodge from here, so two horses were sent on, and Qui-tamer could gallop the ten easily within the hour if necessary, but Tom, who had seemed unusually erratic lately, was determined to enjoy himself on the last day, so Bob Short was to take on his best hunter, and he himself would ride Harkaway to covert as first horse. His last words the evening before were, "Come in good time, old fellow, for Harkaway has a leg! and I value him more than you do Qui-tamer, but we will ride on together as in old times."

Anything to oblige a dear old friend; so next morning breakfast was half an hour earlier, and Qui-tamer cantered over the familiar route to Dale Lodge. The open gate and hoof-marks showed that the hunter had gone on; but what meant that rapid clatter of horse's feet down the carriage drive! Had Tom caught sight of my scarlet coat, and determined to be ready at the gate? No, not likely, for he would never let any one pass without calling. By Jove! it was Harkaway ridden by a stable-helper in shirt sleeves. Hunting-saddle, breast-plate, flask-case, all complete, ready for the field. Had he stolen the horse, or what was the matter? All the helper said, as he galloped out, was "Missus! doctor!"

"Oh, lor! it is four miles along the hard road to the village, and with that leg how will he get there, and what

"MISSIS! DOCTOR!"

will the horse be worth when he gets back?" Poor Tom, too, to lose the last day of the season. He was best left alone, for no good could have been done by calling then, and the sight of a scarlet coat might have had the same effect as on a bull under the trying circumstances. At the meet it was only right to tell Bob Short that he was not likely to be wanted, and had better go home soon, if his master did not come out. We had a glorious run that day, and on the way home it was only friendly to call at Dale Lodge, where Tom was strutting about proud as a peacock, with new dignity as a happy father of a son and heir, and even Harkaway's breakdown did not affect his spirits. "You must be godfather, old fellow, and we will teach the young idea how to ride, soon as he can grip a horse." Poor old Tom! he little knew what was in store for him during the next nine years. Nearly every year his wife presented him with another, and it must have been hard work to find godfathers and godmothers for them all. Gradually, as his family increased, the stud diminished, till now we see him at Selby Gate, ten years after his marriage, with a family of eight, four of them in the wagonette drawn by poor old Harkaway, that had broken down on that fatal day, and been in harness ever since. Now he seemed wearing out, so it was only charity to give Tom the Qui-tamer to take his place, and easy enough to pick up another.

These ten years had been happy enough for me, what with hunting all the winter, and the usual round of pleasure through the summer, but now between the age of thirty and forty something seemed wanting. "Shall I?" was not answered so promptly as formerly, even with Tom's example as a caution, and after all he seemed happy enough, except when he found himself amongst us fellows with no home ties, then he sometimes seemed to yearn for the old free life. After giving him the Qui-tamer it was necessary to look out for another, and the first frost gave an opportunity to run up to Tattersall's. "No. 42, a chestnut gelding, has been ridden and driven" looked likely, but there was a cord stretched behind his stall, and " Dangerous" written up, rather unusual, so he had no admirers, notwithstanding his splendid shape. Dark chestnut, about fifteen hands high, nice short back, long and low, wonderful shoulders, rare clean flat legs, and intelligent head, but a wicked look about the eyes, as if he had been accustomed to be master. A telegram brought Jem Perks up on Monday morning, and he decided to try what could be done, so when the horse came up one bid of twenty guineas bought him. We had a lot of trouble when he first came home, but patience and perseverance worked wonders; and once mastered he turned out the best Qui-tamer of the lot. No day was ever too long for him, hard ground or deep never made his legs fill, and he was rarely in the stable, for he did the work of six. A bad fall that season laid me up for some time, quite a novel experience; but Tom and his wife were most kind, driving over every day with some of the children to amuse the invalid, and Tom rode my horses, so brought home accounts of all that hounds did. Before the season ended, the doctor gave leave for a few days' hunting, and it was a treat to be in the saddle again, but he advised rest and quiet during the summer, and all would be well by next season. No polo, no London gaiety; so time would have been dull if a very pretty, easy-going little hack had not been found; she was a thoroughbred mare, gentle as a lamb, and just perfect. Qui tamer, too, came in most useful, both in the dog-cart and to ride, and it was jolly to saunter about the country, where every field, lane, and wood was familiar. One hot June day the little mare's head was turned towards Dale Lodge, but the usual signal, cracking a whip in the carriage drive brought no response. The family was evidently out; hard lines to go without a cool drink on such a hot morning; where can they be? when a face, and such a face! appeared at the morning-room window. A fresh young face, such as one would expect a fairy to be like, half shy, half smiling, and, yes, in those bright sparkling eyes was a look of amused recognition.

"Good morning, Mr. Selim, (how did she know my name?) Tom has gone out, but will not be long gone, and he left me the keys in case any one called. Will you take anything while you wait for him, for I know he wants to see you." This was said shyly, but with true feminine instinct; she saw her advantage, so I could only stammer—

"You are very kind, so is Tom, but really you have the advantage over me; perhaps Tom told you I might call?"

"No, but we have met before," said she, laughing now, "and the last time you took a liberty and kissed me."

"By Jove! I should like to now," thought I, but could not remember how or when such a pleasant event had happened, and my looks must have expressed my thought, for she said, with perhaps a tinge of disappointment—

"Just like you men, you kiss and you ride away. Do you remember five years ago stopping to pick up a little girl fallen with her pony in a ditch, and you lost a run through it, and looked very cross, though you kissed me and told me not to cry, and you were good to my poor pony, and helped him out of the ditch, till papa came and took me home, but you would not come with him, though it was close by and he asked you? I have often seen you across our place since, and the last time you were leading the field on a brown horse that none of them could catch."

Then the whole scene came vividly before me.

"Well, my dear young lady, you must remember that five years make much more difference in you from the little girl that I dared to kiss, for you did cry so, to what it does in a man getting old."

Luckily Tom and his wife came in, so a formal introduction put matters on a better footing. Miss Gertrude Westonning was a cousin of Tom's wife. After leaving school she had gone abroad to finish her education till the age of nineteen, so that was why we had never met. Pretty was not the word to express her looks, and she sang divinely. Was she still fond of riding? She loved it, and certainly showed to advantage on my little mare. "Shall I?" Qui-tamer must have got tired of always hearing this question on the road home, for he took proceedings himself to bring matters to a climax. It was a broiling hot day in July, too hot to take a young girl out riding, so the mare was left at home, and Qui-tamer jogged over alone.

Tom's tennis-ground was in a meadow near the road, and nearing it, merry voices were heard, and Tom was seen with a great cup to his lips, evidently enjoying himself, for the ice clicked as it was inverted.

"Good health, Tom; leave a little."

"Come quick, then," said he, "or it will be absorbed;" and it seemed so. There was a low stile from the road into the meadow. and Qui-tamer was a good timber-jumper, but he

LIKE A SHOT RABBIT.

did not reckon for the hard slippery ground, so down we came together like a shot rabbit !

A dull thud and a shrill scream, which sounded almost musical, then all was darkness for a time till a confused feeling of comforting soft hands, cool liquid on my burning head, and sweet scent of *eau de Cologne* made me open my eyes to see the most charming sight that ever man beheld. We were alone, while Qui-tamer stood cropping the dry grass close by. The look from those loving, tearful eyes that met mine put life into me again. " Shall I ? " By Jove I did ; nor did I let her go till she had promised to be my wife, extracting a counter-promise that I should never again risk my neck, but hunt quietly and enjoy myself with her.

When Tom came back with an improvised stretcher, that he had been to fetch with a helper, while his wife rushed off to prepare a bed, there was an odd twinkle about his eyes as if he had scored, and his first remark when he saw me get up was—

" I thought if Gertrude could not bring you round you would require this to be carried on, but I am very glad to see you are all right, and when you have had your drink that you were in such a hurry for, you will perhaps be better."

I squeezed his hand, and they helped me in-doors where I stayed for a few days under the best nursing, and, as the truth got abroad, receiving the congratulations of all kind friends.

We were married quietly, and our honeymoon passed pleasantly till the hunting season commenced. Then we came back to the hunting-box—enlarged and improved—with the stud just as it was ; so we have enjoyed the season ; and now that an event is expected, it is Qui-tamer that stands saddled half the day and night with his head where his tail should be, ready to gallop at a moment's notice, for his hard, seasoned legs will not break down on the stoniest road, and so long as our stud is complete, we have no wish to emulate Tom and his wife in any way, while our chief pride is that there is no happier or more devoted couple living than ourselves.

THE BITER BIT.

THE BITER BIT.

"THANK goodness, the county is rid of the old blackguard at last; he's gone back to cockneydom, and will find the backyard of his London house quite wide enough for him—a narrow-minded old humbug."

The speaker was young Tom Reynolds, one of the hardest riding, jolliest young farmers in Gorsefordshire, and we were standing together in the Corn Exchange at Gorseford one market day a few years ago.

"It was not the fault of his neighbours that he did not go long ago," said I. "Whatever brought him down to live in a hunting country, goodness only knows."

The subject of our remarks was an old retired tradesman, whom we may as well call Snooks. He had made a lot of money in London, and was getting on in years, so left his business to his sons to manage, keeping an interest as a sleeping partner, however; while he bought a place in the country to enjoy his *otium cum dignitate*, or "dig a taté," as old Jorrocks has it.

Glastonbury Grange, with one hundred acres of park-like and arable land, and shooting to be had over five hundred more, two packs of foxhounds, a pack of staghounds and harriers, giving opportunities of hunting every day in the week, &c., &c., was advertised for sale down in Gorsefordshire, and Mr. Snooks was the purchaser.

Money will do a great deal. Mr. Snooks, though a rank old Radical at heart, settled down quietly enough as a country gentleman. Neighbours called on him, he gave good dinners, and through the summer (he had come into possession in the spring) all agreed that, though not very sure of his h's, he was not a bad sort for a Londoner, and it was hoped he might prove a pleasant neighbour.

When shooting began he was a great man. Though no shot himself, it was very pleasant to ask his old pals down from town with great *éclat* to have a day's shooting at "my place." But somehow it eked out that he was not over kind to the foxes. The Master of the Foxhounds called on him, and when cub-hunting began the hounds went, as usual, to draw his coverts. They did not do quite so well as usual, much to the disgust of Tom Reynolds, his next neighbour, who, of course, was a staunch supporter of the hunt. Mr. Snooks ventured out on a quiet cob, but riding made him sore and did not suit him, so, having heard a few home truths from Tom, who was out schooling a young one, he set his back up, and would have no more of it. Not that he dared show open enmity to hunting, living as he did in the heart of one of the most sport-loving counties in England; but he determined at the first favourable opportunity to have a row. Hounds were never invited to Glastonbury, which had always been a favourite meet, but as foxes became more and more scarce the Master of the Foxhounds did not care to go there, and as Tom Reynolds could do nothing to mend matters he was at his wits' end.

Though, of course, every one cut the old blackguard he seemed to have a thick hide, and so long as they did not ride over his land, of which he became very particular, he cared little for his neighbours. The staghounds having their game always at hand were independent of him, and as foxes were scarce in his parts stag-hunting became more popular, and many were the good runs enjoyed by its followers. Tom Reynolds was delighted, and gave them a meet whenever they could come there, and as his place joined old Snooks's he gave him a benefit.

Finding that his complaints to the neighbours were of no avail, for of course they only laughed at him, he determined to chance a row and try to stop them, so, though he dared not go so far as to serve notices, he gave orders to his labourers and people that whenever they saw the hunters coming they were to warn them off his land, and, moreover, if any one persisted in coming after such warning they might take other means, hinting that he would protect them in case of assault.

It was not long before the opportunity came. Though turned out ten miles off a deer happened to come that way, and went straight across old Snooks's, without being noticed by two labourers at work in a field. Hounds came along at a good pace, so the leading men with them had jumped into the field before the labourers were aware of it; but they immediately rushed to the gap, armed with their tools, to obey their master's orders. The Master of the Staghounds one of the most popular men in the county, with his huntsman and whips, and a few others in the first flight, went sailing along, without knowing what the labourers meant by their gesticulations, for such antics were unknown in Gorsefordshire; but the pace had been severe, and the distance had told on the field, which showed a considerable tail. Amongst them happened to be Tom Reynolds, riding a raw brute that had lost him a lot of time at his fences, so his disgust may be better imagined than described when he found out the meaning of the sudden stoppage between his own farm and Snooks's.

"What's the meaning of this, Giles?" said he to one of the men who had formerly worked for him, but was better paid by Snooks, who courted popularity in that way.

"Master's orders, sir; no one to cross his land."

"All right, gentlemen," says Tom; "don't let us have a row. Come this way round my place. I'll settle with the old rip after hunting."

But a rough rider, who heard nothing, had meanwhile chosen a fresh place, and got safely over lower down the fence, followed by a well-mounted young stranger, who had been going remarkably well; but his horse being done, the fence was too big for him, and down he came a crasher. Every one else having gone on, he fell an easy prey to the labourers, who marched him off in triumph to the house, thinking, no doubt, to get a great reward from their master for their zeal and cuteness in taking a prisoner. Being hurt and shaken, and his horse dead beat, he gave them little trouble; while, if the truth were known, he was not sorry to have an excuse for being out of the hunt.

MARCHED HIM OFF IN TRIUMPH.

Old Snooks had seen the hunt go by from his study window, fretting and fuming until he saw his men capture their prisoner, and seeing them bring him towards the house, he settled himself in his chair, determined to give such a caution, and make it so unpleasant a prospect for hunting men in future, that he would no longer be subjected to such annoyance, as he expressed it. When a man is in the wrong he never dares look another in the face, so the old beggar had his back to the door when the prisoner was brought in. Making the excuse to be busy writing, he appeared disturbed by their intrusion, and demanded the cause.

"Please, sir, the stag'ounds have been across, and, though we warned 'em, this gent would foller, so we took 'im up, as you told us."

"If he came after you gave notice you should 'ave taken im before the nearest magistrate, not come bothering me," said old Snooks, without looking up, till something made him turn, and he caught sight of his victim; "—— and ——, what made you take him?" said he, seeing that it was one of his largest customers, and the mainstay of the business in London. "Why the —— did not you collar one of the others, you ——?" continued he, quite forgetting that he was a country gentleman.

"So, Mr. Snooks, these men have acted according to your orders?" said the young fellow, quietly. "I heard that you had set up as a country gentleman, but am more than surprised to see the manner in which you carry out the *rôle*. Hunting is one of the few amusements which is within reach of all of us, high, low, rich, and poor. Even cockneys can participate in the enjoyment of the chase; but as we must be as careful of our reputation in the hunting-field as in business, where we are obliged to keep up our credit, you will not be surprised if, after being taken into custody in the field by your orders, I cease to have any further business with the house which bears your name in town."

No apology that the old beggar could offer would alter matters, and it is said that an account of ten thousand a year was transferred to another house; but that would have had little to do with affairs in Gorsefordshire had not the story oozed out. No man can stand ridicule for long, and old Snooks soon got tired of being perpetually laughed at, so took himself back to town. Glastonbury was sold to a rare good sportsman, and has quite retrieved its former prestige as a favourite meet for foxhounds, staghounds, and harriers, and Tom Reynolds is one of the happiest farmers in England in spite of bad times.

WITH ROYALTY ON EXMOOR, 1879.

WITH ROYALTY ON EXMOOR, 1879.

EVER since I first began to follow hounds on a pony years ago, the accounts in the sporting papers of runs with the wild stags in Devon and Somerset have been eagerly read, and the height of my ambition has been to have a day or two with them whenever the opportunity occurred. Year after year something or other has prevented it until last week the long-wished-for day arrived, and now I can not only say that I have hunted in August, but have seen a wild stag killed on Exmoor under circumstances that might never occur again in a lifetime. There are many good fellows, with time and money to spare, fond of nothing but hunting, who would like to have a day or two here if they only knew the way and how to manage, for the present generation do not care to take much trouble even in search of sport, however fond they may be of it.

Thanks to the numerous correspondents who yearly take up their quarters in the West (now, in the year 1885, Lord Ebrington has requested the leading sporting papers not to send special correspondents) sportsmen in other countries are kept well up in all the doings of these hounds; but those who live in the country confine themselves mostly to the actual sport shown without giving much information to strangers who intend to visit them as to the best way of getting about the country and the accommodation to be found there for man and horse; so, as we managed very comfortably, I will give a slight sketch of our travels, besides doing my best to describe the run on Friday, though it would take the work of three special correspondents rolled into one to do proper justice to the latter, what with the immense crowd assembled to greet the Prince, and the almost impossibility of following hounds across the moors in their present heavy state, so as to see all that went on.

Reading a run and following it out on a good map gives one a tolerable idea of the position of meets, coverts, &c., with regard to towns, villages, and railway stations most convenient for reaching them; but only practical experience will teach one how to cross a country and get about, so to a stranger a good pilot is invaluable, and in travelling, of course, a good companion is everything; so my delight may be imagined, when while staying with Mr. Rawle at Berkhampstead, and asking his advice about going, he not only offered to accompany me, but undertook to find horses and manage everything, which, being a native of that country, and as well-known and respected in that land of sportsmen as in our own country, it need not be said that he duly carried out his promise, and we had a very merry time. It was a happy thought of his to write to Exeter to secure horses, for, in anticipation of the Royal visit, they were at a premium, and every available animal nearer the favoured district had been bespoken days before. However, Mr. John Strong (late Pedrick) of Exeter promised to mount us, so all we had to do was to pack a few necessaries in the smallest possible space in saddle-bags to fasten on the saddle so as to make us thoroughly independent, and off we started by an express train on Wednesday, the 20th, prepared to rough it, and in your interest, Mr. Editor, determined to make the best use of my time, and to see as much as possible of the country and its sporting inhabitants, besides taking part in the sport of Friday.

It was deplorable to see the floods out and the mixture of hay and water all the way down the line; but the weather cleared on our arrival at Exeter, and we proceeded at once to inspect our mounts, after which we strolled off to the Horse Bazaar to look through the stables of Messrs. Pedrick and Brice, where we found a lot of hunters, hacks, and match teams, besides a lot of valuable horses in their other stables and loose-boxes outside the town. The presiding genius, Mr. Jack Evans, who is well known, having hunted Lord Poltimore's Hounds for some years, very kindly offered me a mount for Exmoor. I had seen the little horse in the stables up above, and it was very tempting, but having already a mount I was obliged to decline.

On Thursday morning we took our horses by an early train to Taunton, which is the best station for any one intending to hunt from London, for Mr. White lives there, and in ordinary times can find mounts, which can be taken by rail or road to any meet with the Devon and Somerset, but he told us that every animal in his yard was let for the great day, and he did not know whether he should be able to go himself. A kindly hint from him that we should have difficulty in getting quarters anywhere in well-known villages made us choose a quiet spot, so our horses were taken off at East Anstey, some distance from the meet, but close to Mr. Froude-Bellew's kennels, which I was very anxious to see, as the B. B. H. is indebted to him for our little favourite, Bribery, that many good men who have followed them declare to be the best staghound bitch of her size in England, and Nancy, the yellow and white bitch that is so good at hunting in water when a deer takes to a stream. I have also seen some very smart little ones in other kennels, and was very anxious to see the pack which could afford to draft them. Mr. Bellew was busy, but after giving us a capital luncheon and some good advice as to our future conduct and guide to health, he kindly sent his feeder to show us the hounds, and it was no surprise to see a wonderfully smart, level pack of thirty couple bitches and seven couple dogs. Would that we could have a day with them, for the natives say it is wonderful to see them find a fox, and though those wild-bred ones take a lot of killing, it must be an extraordinary one to get the better of the Squire and his pack.

Our horses being fed, we trotted gaily on across moors and up and down steep lanes with high banks covered with wild strawberries, raspberries, and whortleberries, through a beautiful country to the little village of Withybpool, where we took up our quarters for the night at the Oak Tree Inn, about eight miles from the meet next day at Hawkcombe

Head. "The mussiful man is mussiful to his beast," as old Jorrocks says, so our first care was for our horses, and we soon had them comfortably stabled. Determined to rough it, our quarters were none so bad, and with a light heart one does not stick at trifles, so we made the best of everything, for after all the troubles and vexations of the long summer months were we not really going hunting to-morrow.

It seemed almost too good to be true, and after a slight repast (it was not exactly dinner, tea, or supper, but just a pig's chop boiled, with cheese to follow, and a dessert of whortleberries, washed down with bottled ale) we had one more look at our horses, and retired early to rest, but not to sleep, for who can before the first day of hunting? The wind blew a gale down the valley, and rain dashed against our window, but towards morning it cleared, and turned out a glorious day. We were up betimes, and after the morning tub, which we were lucky enough to procure, a visit to the stable showed both horses feeding and looking bright and well. We sat down to breakfast at seven o'clock, and all shortcomings of the evening meal were amply atoned for by a delicious repast of Barle trout just caught and plenty of fresh eggs and cream. Making an early start, we soon arrived at Exford, in time to see the kennels before the hounds left. Arthur Heal was dressing, but his son took us in to see several trophies of the Chase. Heads and slots, some of the latter set in silver for inkstands, and one slot mounted with a candlestick had a melancholy interest, for the inscription says it is from the last hind killed by the old pack, after an extraordinary run, before their sad end.

It will take some years to get such another pack together; but they have already done wonders, and a look through the kennel showed us a splendid lot—about thirty couple—of the biggest dog hounds I ever saw. They cannot get bitches big enough, so have none in the kennel. There are some splendid puppies amongst this year's entry, but the fifteen couple picked for to-day are steady old ones, and if not mistaken I spotted one or two that I have seen before in other packs of staghounds. But it was time to jog on towards the meet. No fear of losing the way, for people were flocking from all parts. On horseback, on foot, some had trudged for miles across the moors to see the Prince, others in every description of trap, cart, and waggon. A favourite fashion was to make up a party in a long, low farm waggon, decorated with boughs and flowers like a moving arbour, drawn by a tandem, with a boy on the leader. The more they bumped and jolted the merrier grew the fun. I never saw so many happy faces. Of course there were a few mishaps and breakdowns, but they seemed to be taken as a matter of course. The shafts of a cart broke just in front of us, shooting its load out backwards. A waggon behind stopped as a matter of course to pick them up, though I don't believe they knew them, but made room so that they might not lose the sight. Seeing his party safe the driver of the cart shoved the broken vehicle on one side out of the way, lighted his pipe, mounted the pony, and rode on with us as if nothing had happened.

Arrived at Hawkcombe Head a sight rarely equalled met our delighted eyes. Fancy a wide open moorland, with bold scenery all round, and distant views of the Welsh coast across the Bristol Channel, with light clouds flying over to give light and shadow, the sun shining bright showing up the white sails of the numerous yachts sailing about, and then the meet in the foreground. I have seen large meets with Her Majesty's at Kenton-lane, near Harrow, when 800 horsemen have assembled, and Maidenhead Thicket on an Easter Monday of course draws a crowd; but to-day beats all. Those more accustomed to estimate numbers put them down at 15,000, but I should say more than that on foot and on wheels, and of horsemen when they were on the move altogether I made out between 1,200 and 1,500. They came from all parts, and besides the natives nearly every hunt in England must have been represented, so it is simply impossible for a stranger to give the names of many who were there; but when Arthur Heal on a well-bred chestnut, and his whip George Southwell on a brown, arrived with fifteen couple of hounds at half-past ten and took up their positions on the moor, a knot of sportsmen gathered round them, and, thanks to my companion, I made out Earl Fortescue, Lord Ebrington, Colonel Anstruther Thomson and two daughters from Fife, Mr. and Mrs. Froude-Bellew, Mr. Nicholas Snow, three well-known M.F.H.'s, Colonel Kingscote, Mr. Williams, Captain Stevenson, and Mr. Glasse, but it would require not only a county directory but one embracing half-a-dozen other counties to give names of half who were there. The Master unfortunately was not out, so the treasurer, Mr. S. Warren, took his place. It was amusing to see the occasional stampedes of horsemen across the moor when word passed along that the Prince was coming, but after several false alarms he arrived at a quarter to twelve in an open carriage and four, with postilions in scarlet jackets. In the carriage with the Prince were Prince Louis of Battenberg, Lord Charles Beresford, the Rev. John Russell, and their host, Mr. Luttrell, M.F.H., of Dunster Castle. Out of consideration for the large crowd they good-naturedly drove right round the meet, so as to be seen by all, and received a hearty welcome on all sides, after which they drove rapidly off to a small house to mount their horses, which had been sent on. Trotting back to the moor, we found Heal in Lord Lovelace's big covert tufting with three couple. This was quite a new experience for me, and the sight was one never to be forgotten. Standing on the hill above the covert we could see all that went on, while the royal party and most of the field, surrounded by the crowd from the meet, were above us. It was like a gigantic pic-nic, for luncheon was now the order of the day amongst them, but we were more interested in the tufting, and it was a treat worth living for to stand on that hill overlooking the covert. Though passing clouds threw an occasional shadow, the sun shone brightly, showing up the best of all colours when we caught sight of Arthur's new scarlet flitting through the glades below—shining, too, on the bold headland and sea in the background; but now hounds were getting busier. Arthur and his whip, with one or two who had followed them into covert, were galloping about, and there was something before them that the more practised eyes of the natives proclaimed to be a stag. They did their best to drive him out, and we could now see him dodging about close before them; but it was no use, he would not break, but managed to put up a young stag, which came sailing up towards us. So we jumped into covert to have a view. Hounds were brought along, but he was not their game, so trotted off along a road and across moors to the deer park at Oare, where some warrantable stags had been harboured, and they began tufting again. Those who have

AWKWARD WORK.

only seen the deer parks round home would hardly know what to make of this one, and many would perhaps fail to distinguish it from the surrounding moors; but it is a famous preserve, and hence its name. No sooner were hounds in than several stags were moved. I counted four, and one magnificent stag came sailing along to us, but hounds were too far off for us to see which they laid on. My companion having hunted here often before, knows all about it, and advised me not to go riding to hounds the same as at home, especially amongst such a crowd and with the going so unusually bad on account of the wet, for he said it is too near our season for us to run extra risk in a strange country. So we stayed quietly back while every one else was tearing about hither and thither, some with the tufters and others with the pack. Lookers-on see most of the game after all, and good luck favoured us, for we fell in with a pilot, Mr. Halse, who has hunted this country with foxhounds and harriers, bringing more to hand than any one, one season, and besides this he has hunted forty-two years with the staghounds. Without knowing all this, there was something about the sporting-looking chestnut mare and the correct get-up of her rider, from cap to spurs, that inspired confidence when he offered to show us the way. Trotting along to a steep combe while the hunt was on our right we saw a fine stag that had evidently been hunted taking soil in a stream. He moved off rather stiffly when he saw us, then quickened his pace, running straight towards the pack. From where we stood we saw the hunt turn and go away fast, while another small body of men were flying in pursuit of a few hounds far to the left. Our pilot trotted and galloped us along, keeping inside as hounds ran a circle, so we could see pretty well all that went on. A shepherd with his hat up gave us a help, and seeing his sheep scud away we could make out the stag sailing towards Badgeworthy Wood, hounds close to him going a good pace, and several of the field close up. Our pilot was galloping now, and we had to send them along best pace across the boggy moor, jumping little water-courses, and looking out sharp to avoid extra soft places, till we came to a steep combe. There we saw the stag turn up the stream right to us, with hounds in view. Was ever such luck for one who had never been in the country or seen a wild stag killed? As they came along the bottom we had to ride down the combe, and then lead our horses when it got too steep. This is awkward work with a strange animal, especially when one has a game leg that can't be depended on. I let go twice, and was down, but kind friends helped, and we reached the bottom all right in time to race along in the first flight to see the death.

As the stag came along, we saw that it was the same we had seen before in the other stream. He turned short before the hounds; they drove him up and down the brawling stream. "Who-whoop," they pull him down. Arthur got hold, handed his knife to the Prince, who gave the *coup de grâce*, and as he had never before been on Exmoor they proceeded to blood him in orthodox fashion, which served both to please and amuse him. The kill was in the valley of the Doone, close by the ruins of the famous house referred to in the tale of *Lorna Doone*, and the valley was soon full of men and horses, galloping in from all sides. Some stayed in the narrow path above, others led their horses down to the stream; many were the scramblings and rolls of horse and man down the rocky sides; some had so much impetus rolling down that they crashed through a small stone wall into the stream, much to the astonishment of His Royal Highness and those below. Colonel Anstruther Thomson astonished even the natives by riding his horse down where some were afraid even to lead. It was half-past four when they killed, and horsemen kept coming in for more than half an hour after, till there must have been about 500 in all at the finish. Seeing they had had such a good run I was rather inclined to upbraid my companion for not having been closer to the hounds while running, but when we heard from those who had been there how the Prince had a narrow escape from a bog, how a lady had been in a bog and it took eight men to get her horse out, how grief had been rife amongst them all, and seeing how more than half the field had been thrown out one way or another, he shut me up and turned the laugh the other way with this speech, "You might have gone if you liked, and got bogged, too ; but now look here, here be the stag, here be the hounds, here be the Prince, and here be WE!" Besides this, our horses were comparatively fresh, while others looked considerably done. We crossed the stream, and wended our way across the moor in the best of company with the hounds nearly to Exford, where we were to turn off for Withypool.

Before leaving them, let me offer a few words of advice to strangers from other hunts who intend to hunt with them. Although the Master, Mr. Fenwick Bisset, contributes mainly towards their maintenance, he has been put to so much extra expense lately, through the loss of his valuable hounds, that, being a subscription pack, it seems hardly fair to hunt with them without contributing something towards the hunt. In the absence of the Master, the treasurer, Mr. S. Warren, takes his place; but as I know from practical experience that it is next to impossible to combine the duties and take notice of every one who is out, intending subscribers should find him out instead of leaving him to ask them. Money spent on hunting is never thrown away, but many men will spend it broadcast for their own convenience, and forget altogether that hounds require money to keep them going. No one has a right to follow hounds often without subscribing something towards their maintenance, and I hope that any sportsman who goes down here on my recommendation to have a few days' hunting before any other packs begin to hunt will remember this hint, and not take it amiss.

After a pleasant ride with the hounds, we said good-bye as they turned off to the kennels, and soon arrived at our quarters at Withypool. Here we should have stopped for the night, but being anxious to get back we retraced our steps the way we came the day before. Crossing the moors and over a country by dark, the instinct of our horses took us right. I love an animal that gets one out of a difficulty, and became quite fond of the good black that had carried me, saddle-bags and all, through the day, and was still game as a pebble. The villages seemed all full of tired men and horses, so we plodded on through the dark, while the lanes seemed to get steeper, with more loose stones about and streams to cross as the horses got tired; and to add to our miseries it rained in torrents at intervals, but one of Woolgar's mackintosh coats and leggings combined kept all dry and warm, till at last we arrived at Dulverton about ten o'clock. This is a rare place to stop, and very convenient for nearly all meets. Though the Lamb and its stabling were full to overflowing, the landlord is a good fellow, and found us stabling and rooms in the town; so after a good supper with him we were well off after all our troubles.

I heard afterwards that the Prince of Wales had a cup of tea and some bread and cheese at Nicholas Snow's of Oare, the Master of the Stars of the West Fox-hounds. Miss Leslie asked Mr. George Luttrell to allow the Prince's carriage to go at a foot pace past her door, as she had the old women of the village collected to see him. When he did pass, the front rank was composed of the belles of the village, who, said H.R.H., were the best samples of old women he had ever seen.

Next morning we returned our horses to Exeter, and were soon on the way home. Never shall I forget the kindness and hospitality shown to us by every one on our journey, or the fun and jollity we enjoyed during our short stay; and if all goes well next year and we do not have another day or two it will not be the fault of the writer.

NOTES ON RIDING TOURS.

NOTES ON RIDING TOURS.

I.

through a large box of old letters, papers, and memorandum books that have accumulated during several years, it was like meeting an old friend to come across a small book of Notes put together during a riding tour in 1871, and further search revealed others, compiled since, that awoke many pleasant reminiscences, with the wish that such a tour could be undertaken again; but this year other engagements prevent it, so, for the benefit of others who may like to set out on horseback, those old note-books contain a few hints that will be useful, and at the same time might amuse other readers, just now, when every one is seeking rest and holiday. Instead of rushing abroad and spending their substance, besides running the risk of contaminating diseases now raging in foreign countries, let Englishmen travel quietly about, and enjoy the beauties of our own country, studying the habits of rural populations, which will be found quite as interesting as those of any foreigners whose language cannot be half understood; our quiet old-fashioned hotels are very comfortable, and a good square meal always obtainable, with ale to wash it down, and very often rare good old wine is to be found in out-of-the-way places; and, what is of most importance, money spent liberally amongst our own people benefits the nation and comes indirectly back to all of us. The public coaches running daily out of London and between many country towns have done a great deal of good in this direction, while the various kinds of human propellers bring long ranges of country within reach; but wheels must keep to the roads, besides entailing a certain amount of hard labour, so the full enjoyment of perfect independence, and at the same time rest, is not obtainable as on horseback.

With a good hack, twenty to twenty-five miles a day can be easily accomplished for a week or more, and no better way for getting a hunter into condition just before hunting could be devised. There is always the chance during September of getting a day amongst the cubs, or if a trip were made to the West in August, a few days with the Devon and Somerset Staghounds might be enjoyed, and in the New Forest both deerhounds and foxhounds are at work.

It is curious that just as these notes were being put in shape, another writer in the magazine last month, in an able paper on "Horse Shows," should have written concerning roadsters. Who nowadays would roll up his other shirt, and stuff it into a wallet, in company with slippers, horse-pick, and perhaps a crust of bread and cheese, preparatory to embarking on a journey by road? The object now is to show how these useful items may be packed with more that may be required for a lengthened tour. Had it not been for the love of touring on horseback those charming books by "The Druid" (the late H. H. Dixon) might not have been written; and now others may like to set out.

For outfit great care should be taken as to a well-fitting saddle that does not shift about with the weight of the saddle-bags. These two, made of soft cow-hide, should be about eleven inches deep by eight and three wide, well balanced on D-rings behind the saddle, with a girth passed through the breastplate to keep them from shaking. Packed carefully, they will hold a light covert coat in case of wet— Gray and Botthamley, of Grantham, for choice—a pair of thin trousers, two flannel shirts, a few white washing ties that take the place of collars, three pairs of socks, pocket-handkerchiefs, a pair of tennis slippers that do for out-door wear, and a dressing-case that measures $6\frac{1}{2}$ by $3\frac{1}{2}$ inches. A pair of thin waterproof leggings can be strapped in front of the saddle, in a case that is also handy for holding small articles or luxuries. A short curved briar pipe that cannot be jammed down your throat is best for smoking, as cigars take up so much room, and tobacco can always be obtained, while they cannot. Breeches and gaiters will be found most comfortable, and easier to walk in when necessary than boots. A light hunting-whip is a capital companion to keep cur-dogs in order and ensure civility amongst small boys, on whom the thong has a wonderful moral effect. A map and compass will be useful; Stanford's reduced Ordnance are best, but Phillips's county maps are handy for the pocket. Great care must be taken in packing the saddle-bags to balance them exactly, and they should weigh seven pounds each, filled with every necessary for a ten-stone man on a month's tour. There is a new metal, Webster's patent aluminium, for bits, stirrups and spurs, which are to be bought at Garden's, 200, Piccadilly, and will be found invaluable where saving time and labour is an object, as they only require washing and drying with a leather to shine like silver, and they ought never to wear out, as there is no burnishing required. A trial has proved this, and they give great satisfaction in many stable-yards. Companions on these tours must be well chosen, and—more important still—horses must travel well together at even paces, or the trip is best undertaken alone. In this respect our first start, on August 21, 1871, was most happy.

Mounted on a thoroughbred chestnut hunter, with a brother on an equally well-bred black mare, that could keep evenly together at any pace, we reached St. Albans in time for luncheon, and climbed the Abbey Tower to see the view; then jogged on to the Hertfordshire kennels in time for tea with Ward, who showed us the hounds and horses; then sent our horses on to Luton, and drove us in the evening to " The George," where we found comfortable quarters for the night. A nice place is Luton, and lively. Next morning we rode along the high road, with broad turf on either side, to Barton, getting a grand view from the hills and a nice breeze; but down below the heat was scorching, and we were glad to reach Silsoe, where we stabled our horses, and lay under the trees in Wrest Park till it became cooler, and we started for Bedford, passing great fields of onions, which turned our ideas towards steaks; and we did enjoy them at "The Swan," where the art of amalgamation of these choice comestibles was well understood. That evening the heat was choking, so we sauntered to the bathing-place, and revelled in the water exhibition, for the Bedford boys are amphibious. A thunder-storm at night cooled the air, but unsettled the weather, so, instead of visiting the Oakley kennels as we had intended, we put on our waterproofs and jogged on to Newport Pagnell, where, being market day, we listened to a comical auctioneer selling sheep; he was a wag, and kept his audience in a roar, while prices seemed to run high. It rained hard as we went to Stony Stratford, and at the hotel there was only a commercial room, so, like the bagmen of old, we unpacked our goods, and mystified the inhabitants, who did not know what to make of us—perhaps they took us for highwaymen; but we were made most comfortable, and the charges were very moderate. Next morning it rained again in torrents and blew hard, disappointing us of our intended visit to Wakefield Lawn, for a wet day on the flags is not enjoyable, so we rode on, hoping that it would clear before we reached Whaddon Chase; but we met Squire Lowndes's hounds out at exercise close to their kennels, then rode on to Leighton Buzzard, where it was intended to stop; but the day was still young, and the rain cleared off, so after a bait we jogged on to Mentmore, where Fred Cox showed us the hounds, and after tea poor Barker took us round the late Baron's stables, which contained as fine a stud as is now to be seen at Ascot.

No one ever looks at the time when with hounds and

horses, so it was late and rained in torrents as we reached Tring, where young Sam Brown always welcomes sportsmen, and knows how to make them comfortable when coming home wet or weary to the Royal Hotel. A chat with John or Sam Brown, who are full of sporting recollections during the last eighty years, is always a treat; and if Herbert is at home, he can keep the game alive all round.

Friday was a grand summer's day, bright but cool, and very clear for getting long views, so we thoroughly enjoyed the ride to Berkhampstead, where we paid our respects to Mr. Rawle, the worthy Master of the Buckhounds, who showed us his smart little ladies, and gave us some good advice before we started for Bricket Wood, through which and by familiar by-paths we rode home, having travelled rather more than 100 miles during the five days.

The next tour was undertaken alone on the same chestnut horse; he was an odd-tempered animal, and always went much more pleasantly by himself than in company. To save time in getting to the country in which we wished to travel, we took train to Dorking, and started on August 16, 1873, a few days after the fatal accident to the Bishop of Winchester, who had been riding near Evershed's Rough. Riding through this country, the scenery is so beautiful that no one would wonder at a horseman being so engrossed that he grew careless, and left his horse to saunter on; but the small cross, cut in the turf at the exact spot, showed plainly where the slight hollow caused the accident. St. Margaret's Church, on the hills above Guildford, was a familiar landmark by which to steer for a hospitable mansion, where many pleasant days have been enjoyed. There luncheon and plenty of chaff was ready for the wayfarer, who started refreshed through Wonnersh and Godalming to Haslemere, to spend Sunday. On Monday, a moorland ride by Hind Head and the Devil's Leap to Farnham, and through Aldershot, Farnborough, and Frimley, to Bagshot on a soaking wet afternoon, so put up at an old-fashioned inn, with great stables that told of the glory of the road in days gone by.

It was fine next morning, and the pinewoods smelt fresh towards Ascot, where a visit was of course paid to the Royal Kennels. Goodall was away; but Bartlett showed the hounds, and they had a good entry that year.

Rode on to Binfield for luncheon, and by a short cut, which sadly disconcerted the owner of the beautiful park, till a message was delivered by way of explanation, and he was much entertained with the conceit, and also the mode of travelling. Haines Hill was the destination, and a pleasant hour spent looking over Mr. Garth's hounds with Brackley, who after tea put us in the way by a very pretty road through Twyford and Wargrave to Henley, in time for stewed eels at the "Red Lion." There was a local regatta next morning, and plenty of fun on the river, so a late start was made to Maidenhead and Windsor, where there is always plenty to see, so the afternoon was spent in the Royal Mews and going round the Castle. After a wet night, the clear view from the Round Tower was well worth the arduous climb. Harrow, Highgate, Hampstead, and the Crystal Palace could be seen, also St. Alban's Abbey, and of course the Buckinghamshire scenery. The journey this day was through Datchet to Langley, where a visit was paid to Sir Robert Harvey's (late the Prince of Wales's) Harriers, a pretty little pack, that not only hunt their own game, but give good account of any deer that they are laid on. George Farr was naturally proud to show them; also the horses, which were a good lot. A relative's house at Hillingdon was the destination that night, and next morning, as usual, an early visit was paid to the stable. While feeling the old horse's legs, a sharp nip from his teeth in the fleshy part of the shoulder warned that something had upset him, for, awkward as he was with strangers, he had always been civil to his owner, and even now seemed ashamed of himself when he found that he had made a mistake. A great clattering of horse's feet on the stones outside, accompanied by loud objurgations, showed that the qui-tamer of the establishment was being dressed, and the groom was operating on his thick hide with a besom. "Did you dress this one with that machine?" "Oi troied, but 'ee wouldn't let me; and you had better feed 'im yourself, and put yer saddle on, for 'ee won't let me near 'im." And no wonder with a thoroughbred skin to be insulted like that. That morning was lovely and jolly, to ride through Ruislip, Pinner, and the glorious Harrow country home, where we were busy hunting with Draghounds that season, and had rare gallops over the grass round Barnet and Totteridge. The beauty of our home counties in summer time is little known even to Londoners, who live so near. These quiet tours in Surrey, Herts, and Middlesex are within reach of numbers who only want a lead to show them the way. As to cost, one pound a day covers expenses of man and horse if economy is a matter of importance, while there is more enjoyment to be had for this money than if spent rushing about by train, or doing nothing at seaside places. Those sportsmen who do not keep horses can hire useful hacks for a tour along the South Coast, from

OPERATING WITH A BESOM

Dupont of Brighton, or, in the West of England, from John White of Taunton, English of Cheltenham, and John Strong of Exeter. Near London, Harveyson of Finchley has always strong hacks fit to go, so have John Read of Watford, and Flack of Stevenage. Besides these two tours, others have been made on horseback.

II.

THE first paper on this subject appeared, two or three letters have been received from ladies asking why no advice was given to them how to pack saddle-bags and accompany their husbands or brothers on riding tours; so, the desire to please the fair sex being the highest motive of man, every care has been taken to afford the required information. Not an easy matter for a bachelor to accomplish, and many might have been daunted by the apparent hopelessness of giving satisfaction, for how can a man know the requirements of a lady on tour? Still, the desire to please obliged the subject to be undertaken systematically, and it is hoped that the result will give satisfaction. The first thing was to find a saddle-bag suitable for a side-saddle, so a visit was paid to Mr. Smith,

151, Strand, the Colonial saddler and outfitter, who has a waterproof canvas bag, eighteen inches by twelve, and expanding six, which hangs to D rings on the off side of the saddle with straps also to the girths to prevent shaking. The next thing was to try how much could be packed into it, and now came the working of a master mind. With a large acquaintance among the fair sex it was not difficult to choose three practical young ladies to whom a prize (a box of chocolate) was offered for the best solution to the problem, and who should also give a list of what could be packed, which is as follows:—A thin silk dress, flannel undergarment, sleeping requirements, stockings (silk takes up least space), pocket-handkerchiefs, tennis slippers, brush and comb, etc., etc.; so it is to be hoped that etc., etc., comprises all the little necessary accessories to their toilet of which we men know nothing. The practical fair one (who well deserved that box of chocolate) also suggests the use of "ever clean" collars and cuffs, which are made of specially prepared waterproof linen, that can be washed with soap and water and dried with a towel, ready to be put on every morning. A light mackintosh, with a skirt to protect the whole habit, can be rolled up in front of the saddle, and a light coloured billycock hat with veil should be worn. Thus equipped a lady might travel for a few days, but if a lengthened tour was undertaken it would be best to have a groom driving with the luggage in a dogcart, which would also be available in case of fatigue or wet weather. With such an auxiliary parties might be formed, say a few young people with a sedate chaperone in the dogcart to meet them in the evening with the rest of the heavy baggage; nor would it be a bad way of spending the honeymoon, especially if the old-fashioned pillion of our ancestors was revived.

But for real enjoyment in travelling there is nothing to equal horseback, and it is to be hoped that many will profit by these hints, and see the beauties of our country, instead of rushing about abroad by sea and railway.

Now, to continue with personal reminiscences, by far the most pleasant tour yet undertaken was in 1876. That year the end of the hunting season will be always remembered by the awful snow-storms that stopped hunting in April, when the deep lanes were so blocked that we could not even get to a meet. It was out hunting in a snow-storm that a bad cold was caught, and a long period of easterly winds afterwards gave no chance of recovery, till kind friends and doctors grew anxious and recommended change of air with total rest, so how could that be better obtained than on a riding tour? It was on June 21st that saddle-bags were packed, and the journey to London accomplished in time to take train from Waterloo to Portsmouth—a blazing hot day, when it was pleasant to find comfortable quarters at the Queen's Hotel, Southsea, while the good little bay mare was stabled at Hutchins's, where it was seen that every attention would be paid to her, while there was yet time for a walk to explore the town, and enjoy the cool breeze on the pier. Here was a tragedy when the Isle of Wight boat came in, for an old lady slipped off the landing-board into the water, followed by a railway porter and two other officials, who dived in and effected a gallant rescue, while women fainted, and a pickpocket of course improved the occasion to ply his craft; but no sooner was his hand in somebody else's pocket, than he was collared by a lynx-eyed limb of the law, and as we bystanders made a cap for the plucky divers, we saw them form a procession with their salvage and her rejoicing relatives, followed by the crestfallen pickpocket led off to durance vile between two stalwart Hampshire constables.

Intending to cross over to the Isle of Wight next day, it was necessary to get information as to the ferry-boat for the mare, which was soon arranged, and there was a capital Show of Dogs, Poultry, etc., to visit before dinner.

Next morning an early start was necessary to catch the ferry-boat, and soon after seven we were under way. Luckily it was a cool, calm morning, with the sea like glass, so we were ferried over to Ryde by 9.30. As the sun got high, it was a hot ride to Newport, where a shower of rain cooled the air, while we called at Marvell, where Mr. Harvey then kept the foxhounds. They were out at exercise ; but it was a short ride back to Carisbrook for luncheon, and a ramble round the Castle, with its famous well and historical associations ; after which we went down to the kennels again, just as hounds came in, and spent a pleasant half-hour with the Master. On the way to Sandown a visit should have been paid to Mr. Frank Barton, who kept a pack of harriers, but rain came down in torrents, so the mare trotted on to Sandown, and we were made comfortable at the Royal Hotel. Next morning after a jolly bathe, for there is no place to beat Sandown Bay for a swim, there were old friends to visit, and old haunts to see before starting for an undecided haven—for this is the beauty of travelling on horseback, you can stop where you take a fancy; so rode on through Shanklin, where the way was enlivened by a bright little boy on a grey pony, who knew all about hunting in the district, and gave good advice as to quarters for the night. It was a lovely ride through Bonchurch and Ventnor, past St. Lawrence to the Sandrock Hotel; but that seemed too far from the sea for a bathe.

There was a toll-bar on the way, tenanted by one of the prettiest turnpike keepers ever seen, with a bright smile for the payee, who stopped for change. Here is a hint for road surveyors and trustees: re-establish the turnpikes with such pretty keepers, when not only will all the amateur mashers take to the road on bicycles or tricycles, but they will be anxious that payment should be compulsory for all their fraternity, so the roads could be kept in order without appealing to the rates.

These reflections occurred on the road to Blackgang, where we put up at the Chine Hotel for the night. At the foot of the Chine was quite a romantic spot for a bathe at high water, after which and a good breakfast it was a jolly ride along the new government road by the cliffs to Freshwater, where the principal hotel is in the hands of Mr. Lambert, a sportsmen fond of hunting; so, needless to say, mare and rider were made comfortable for Sunday, while his knowledge of hunting and anecdotes thereon were most entertaining. There is much to see in the neighbourhood, and it is a popular resort for young couples on their honeymoon. The difficulty was how to avoid them, for they do scowl so on a lonely bachelor with a twinkling eye, who comes suddenly upon them in quiet corners, while seeking seclusion for himself. In the beautiful garden round the hotel were loving couples, on the seashore were loving couples, high up at the Beacon on the Downs was a loving couple, down at Alum Bay a loving couple landed off a yacht, and on the way back to the hotel it was very hard lines to be driven out from a shady nook, which was really meant to enjoy a pipe in, by a scowling young couple who evidently considered it their own and desecrated by a smoker; so it was given up to them, and in sheer desperation a seat was chosen

HINT FOR ROAD SURVEYORS.

on the open downs, so that young couples might see from a long distance what to avoid, and if they came that way it was their own fault. After dinner it was noticed that most of the bridegrooms amalgamated for a social smoke, leaving their respective brides to their own devices. They were not so sociable, for there were two sitting at the opposite ends of the long dining-table writing what were evidently the first letters home to mamma, saying how they liked the married state—a labour involving deep study and much concentration of thought, judging by the corresponding contraction of brows into wrinkles. Enter their affectionate bridegrooms much concerned to note those anxious faces. One who must have been a wag was apparently about to send a chaffing message, when he suddenly remembered that the kind, considerate lady, who had so often helped him in many different ways during his courtship, was now his mother-in-law, and at the awful thought his cheek paled, and he shut up like a telescope.

On the Monday morning it was a short ride to Yarmouth, where the ferry-boat was ready to start for the mainland. In company with a gipsy van and three horses, it was a rough passage till the steamer reached the river and proceeded up its course, marked out by fir-trees like a boulevard into Lymington, where it was some satisfaction to be once more on *terra firma*. Then a visit was paid to Mr. Cooper's Stud Farm, for the nephew of the late Captain Billy Cooper of road fame keeps one of the best appointed stables in the country. Then the beauties of the New Forest were enjoyed through Brockenhurst, where the first acquaintance was made with the dreaded forest flies. A white pony turned out from his stable into the forest to graze commenced to run about kicking like mad, and while laughing at his antics without knowing the cause, a loose seat on the usually quiet little bay mare nearly brought about a catastrophe when she suddenly made a bolt, kicking and bucking as if to get rid of her rider, saddle-bags and all; nor did she settle down till Lyndhurst was reached, and at the Crown Hotel Stables the mystery was solved by the ostler, who proceeded to take off the flies at great risk of getting kicked. In those days the present genial host of the Crown, Mr. Palmer, had not appeared; but Mr. Loman, the proprietor, managed to get a bed in the village, for the hotel was full during a cricket week, and there was plenty of fun in the pretty little village. After dinner there was time for a walk to the foxhound kennels, and a talk with merry Charles Hawtin, who has since joined the majority, and is buried with his father and brother at Emery Down close by. Next morning there was another beautiful ride through the Forest to Romsey, and on to the Hursley Kennels, where we stayed so late talking to Alfred Summers, that all thoughts of where to sleep were forgotten, and it was nine o'clock when the Royal Hotel at Winchester was reached, to find that with Stockbridge Races, the Militia in training, and Assizes on, all at the same time, beds and stabling were at a premium. However, we found a room, and, after supper, slept the sleep of the just. Next day the heat was scorching as we went over the Downs, and by pretty lanes to the Hambledon Kennels at Exton, where we saw Mr. Walter Long's pack with Alfred Mandeville, and then rode on through a thunderstorm to the Anchor at Ropley, where Bailey, father of the two well-known huntsmen, was quite sorry that he was alone in the house, with no woman left to cook; but after seeing the mare comfortable, he cooked two splendid chops, two great rashers of home-cured bacon, and two eggs, apologising for not getting more; but though dinners have been partaken at the Mansion House and in many famous temples of gastronomy, no meal was ever better enjoyed, and when over a pipe he began to tell anecdotes we passed a very pleasant evening. Next morning the storm had cooled the air, so, after a visit to Mr. Deacon's kennels close by, we set out through Alton to Farnham, where kind friends made us welcome. For the next few days, what with visits to Aldershot, fishing in Frensham pond, and a look at Mr. Coombe's hounds in their new kennels, time slipped by till Monday, when a lovely ride along the Hog's Back, with those grand views on either side, took us to Guildford, and other pleasant quarters for the night. Then a long ride next day through Woking, Chertsey, Hampton and Twickenham to Isleworth late at night, and on home the following day, having spent three weeks pleasantly with much benefit to mare and rider. Steady travelling hardens horses' legs and of course does good to condition, while as for a horseman the perfect rest and enjoyment with the feeling of freedom and independence does more good than would be believed by many until they try it.

The next time the saddle-bags were packed it was more with the object of a ride round about home than a long tour. On the 10th August, 1877, the old chestnut hunter journeyed down to the Rose and Crown, Watford, and we started next morning for Shendish, paid a visit to Bob Worrall, who showed us the Old Berkeley hounds, then jogged on to Berkhampstead, where Mr. Rawle was busy harvesting, but made us welcome to spend Sunday; and a happy day it was, for the Master of the Buckhounds is a genial host, and at that time arrangements were made which have since turned out happily. On Monday morning it was a delightful ride to the Hertfordshire

Kennels at Kennesbourne Green, and, after luncheon with Ward, we jogged on to Stevenage, and put up at Flack's Yorkshire Grey. Next day rode to Hitchin, attended market, and round to Bendish, where we stayed a few days, and rode home through Hatfield. Many short rides have been taken since, and the saddle-bags are always ready for the road. During September, when the days get cooler and cub-hunting commences, there is much pleasure in riding about from kennel to kennel, sleeping handy to the early meets, and after a morning amongst the cubs riding on to see another pack, and perhaps hunting with them next morning. What a lot of sport could be enjoyed in Devonshire just now by taking two horses, with a light lad to ride the one carrying the saddle-bags! they could hunt alternate days, and, always having the bags handy, no longer distances need be travelled after hunting, but just sleep at the nearest place. In this way we once enjoyed a visit to the west, and hope others will try it.

BRICKET WOOD.

BRICKET WOOD.

that has hunted from London does not know this famous stronghold for foxes? a neutral covert, drawn by the Hertfordshire and the Old Berkeley Hounds that hunt this part of the country alternate months. Situated midway between Watford and St. Alban's, with the branch of the London and North-Western Railway running through its centre, it is easily accessible by rail, while, given a good hack, it is quite possible to send on a hunter in the morning and ride down from "the little village." With what different feelings do the members of either hunt notice this fixture on their cards or hunting advertisements. The keen ones, who know their way about it and how to get out quickly when hounds go away, knowing well the chance they have of getting a run, will exclaim, "Dear old Bricket!" and keep their best horses—two, if possible—to make sure of being in a run; while others, who only think of the deep-holding rides and a few awkward fences that may throw them out, say, "Bricket again? Confound the place! Any old screw, and the worst clothes in the wardrobe, will do *for that!*" Bricket Wood, with the Scrubs and coverts adjoining, consists of about 1000 acres. These are Burston's and Blackboy Wood and coverts on Mr. Hibbert's estate at Munden, which join the Scrubs. Also Mr. Hegan's covert at Bucknall's, where foxes make their home. With so much covert, and most of it, especially the Scrubs and Bricket Wood, itself very thick, it is not easy to force a fox away; but of late, being constantly hunted, they have been taught to fly, and sport has much improved in consequence.

Each pack has a separate meet when Bricket Wood is on the card. The Hertfordshire meet at the cross-roads near the Noke, on the St. Alban's and Watford Road, two miles from the former; while the Old Berkeley meet at the Old Toll Bar, nearer Watford. Both packs meet at Mr. Hibbert's, Munden House, on the opposite side of the wood, nearer Aldenham, and at Newberries; and the Old Berkeley have met at Bucknall's, and often draw here from Bushey Mill. From the Hertfordshire meet hounds commence drawing Burston's, while the field, generally a large number of horsemen, make their way up the lane leading to the railway station, waiting till they draw round to Blackboy Wood, and Bob Ward has been known to slip away with a fox to Gorhambury before any but a few knowing ones found out they were away. Then, in the Scrubs, how often the field has been caught napping; and, again, from the thick-lying brambles in Bricket, where a fox has jumped out and gone straight to Mr. Solly's Serge Hill coverts, and the luckiest horsemen, who have had a real stern chase, just managed to catch sight of the leaders riding to hounds running hard to the Grove or Cassiobury Park. The Old Berkeley go from the Old Toll Bar direct to these thick-lying brambles, and a fox will then make for the Scrubs, cross the railway to Munden, then across the River Colne to Aldenham Abbey or Berry Grove, near Bushey Hall. Then they get on to the grass, and they have been known to run to Newberries and Combe Wood, near Shenley. From Munden House hounds draw the little covert towards the Scrubs, then the said Scrubs, and here it is well for their followers to be careful. The narrow paths between the thick bushes are deep and slushy, as the ground is quite undrained, and broken or freshly-cut stubbs, sharp as a razor, will very soon lame a horse. The best way is to take the road, such as it is, to the railway, over the bridge to the brickfield, through this, and over a little post and rails on to the high bridge, from which the whole of the Scrubs can be seen. If a fox goes away towards Munden the same route may be retraced, but if he crosses the railway there is a solid path which may be followed to the road which divides the wood, and whichever way hounds turn they can be caught. Again, suppose he breaks for Bucknall's, there is a solid path through the brickfield, and away past the house to Garston's, if the fox goes for the Gullet. The best way to enjoy Bricket, and, in fact, all great woods where there is difficulty in getting away, is to have two horses out, with a second horseman who can be depended on to wait quietly outside without chattering and heading a fox. Then, as you come galloping out with the first half-blown, you get on the fresh one and sail away. But it is always more satisfactory even to be left behind in covert than to get too forward and head a fox. You can always make up for lost time, but no one gets over the disgrace when he is to blame for a fox being chopped. Hard lines on huntsmen and whips, when they have had all the trouble of getting a fox to the open, to see him turn short back, and hounds run into him, because some jealous fool is anxious to get a start. But how often this has happened in Bricket, and many a good fox has come to an unsatisfactory end!

Bricket is not famous as a game covert, and Mr. Bailey, of Cuckman's, rented it for some years as a fox covert, for he rarely shot there, and during his time hounds rarely drew blank. Some rare runs were enjoyed there, and also from Park Wood and Birch Wood to Gorhambury. Pre Wood, too, held foxes that would run to Bricket, and now they do the same. When Mr. Hibbert, of Munden, took the shooting he had trouble at first, and Bricket almost lost its reputation; but now, under the care of a keeper who came with a certificate from a M.F.H., the right animal predominates, and blank days are unknown. Some of the best days enjoyed during late years may be given as they are jotted down in an old diary.

January 28, 1878. Bricket Wood, O.B.H. Soaking wet

day; found leash of foxes; hounds divided; both lots ran well in different directions; no kill.—February 22, 1878. Herts. Found brace, perhaps changed during run; but killed old dog-fox after capital run in Cassiobury Park.— March 11. O.B.H. chopped fox in covert.—23rd. O.B.H. met at Newberries; Mr. Longman hunting them. Found in Bricket Scrubs, ran forty minutes to Gorhambury.— February 7, 1879. Herts. Wet day after severe frost; bad riding. Found at once in Bricket; lost him near Aldenham. Found again in Pre Wood, ran to Gaddesden; lost near Water End.—February 28. Herts. Good run, and killed. Good run from Stroud Wood, afternoon,—March 10. O.B.H. Found in Bricket; lost him. Found in Serge Hill, ran to Pre Wood, on through Batch Wood to Harpenden Common, and left him.—March 31. Ran one to Cassiobury, and another to Gorhambury,—April 18. Herts. Nice little run; no kill.—October 22, 1879. Herts. Ran one to ground at Serge Hill. Good run with another to King's Langley.— January 12, 1880. O.B.H. Bucknall's. Killed one, ran other to Pre Wood.—February 6. Herts. Ran to Newberries and Shenley.—March 8. O.B.H. King's Langley Station; drew to Bricket; found brace, short runs, and killed two.— March 22. O.B.H. lost the first, ran second to ground, killed the third.—November 29, 1880. O.B.H. ran fast to Park Street, Hedge's Farm, and killed in garden at St. Albans. Found other at Abbot's Hill, and whipped off at dark.— January 10, 1881. O.B.H. Bushey Mill. Ran one to ground at Aldenham Abbey. Ran another from Bricket to Gorhambury Fish Ponds, and killed.

The season just passed has been the best ever remembered by frequenters of Bricket, both packs having had good runs, and it has never been drawn blank. Twice the O.B.H. have run to Whippendale, and when meeting near Lord Clarendon's, they ran back and killed their fox at Bedmond on his way to Bricket. The Hertfordshire one day ran a fox to ground near St. Alban's, and another to Abbot's Langley. Altogether about six brace of foxes have been accounted for from Bricket and its vicinity. Right well has it regained its former reputation, showing what can be done. Would that some other covert owners in Hertfordshire would follow Mr. Hibbert's example, for at the present time there are few keepers who could gain a certificate from an M.F.H. Notably on the west side of the country there are some once-famous fox coverts, which are now always drawn blank. Not only are there no foxes, but covert-side gossips say that out of two thousand pheasants, hand-reared and turned down, only six hundred were shot. What became of the rest only Mr. Keeper knows, and his master would no more question him about them than about foxes. The days of big battues are passing, and covert owners find out how they have been robbed to supply the markets. May long life and good sport be the lot of those who see the error of their ways, and may all good keepers, who know how to keep foxes and pheasants, get places where they will be appreciated. When another season finds Bob Ward and Bob Worrall alternately rousing the echoes in dear old Bricket may there be plenty of the right animals, and the coverts will sustain their ancient reputation so well regained this season.

Since the above was written for *Baily's Magazine* in July, 1882, "dear old Bricket" has well sustained its reputation.

On September 26th, 1882, the Old Berkeley met at Munden, at half-past six, and with thirty-one and a-half couples of nippy ladies, Bob Worrall was soon busy with a strong litter, bred in the garden. They were found in the Scrubs; and a field of about twenty horsemen cut off their retreat, so hounds spent an hour merrily chasing the little rascals with a rare scent, and such a crash of music, till they brought one to hand, and enjoyed an early breakfast in spite of the heat, which was by this time choking, as the sun got up.

On November 6th, the O.B.H. met at Munden again, and the lesson learnt during cub-hunting, that the cubs would make for their home in the garden, enabled some of us to see a brace killed after short sharp scurries from the Scrubs, when only the chosen few got away on terms with the nippy ladies. Then came a clipper in the afternoon, from Black Green Wood away by the Old Toll Bar to the gorse and Winch Hill Wood, racing to Serge Hill, where Mr. Solly's litter of cubs diverted the attention of hounds, till Mr. Longman viewed the old stager away, when twelve and a-half couples came to his horn with a few lucky horsemen, to see them race back to Bricket, where the whipper-in holloaed him over the road to Black Green Wood, and they drove him through Burston's, out across Col. Bigg's Park, over the road where they were brought to their noses, and Bob Worrall hit him off towards Gorhambury; but a storm came on, so scent failed, and that fox well deserved to save his brush.

On the 10th, the Hertfordshire met at Gorhambury, and had a real good day in Pre Wood, Park Wood, Birch Wood, and Serge Hill to Bricket, but did not kill a fox.

On the 27th the O.B.H. met at Bushey Mill, but did not find till they got to Bricket with this result :—

I stood on the bridge at noontide,
    As Bob Worrall was drawing the Scrubs,
And his hounds spread out like demons,
    To find the wily cubs.

Then I saw his orange jacket
    In the ploughed field far away,
Like a golden goblet shining—
    "We'll never catch him to-day."

And far in the hazy distance,
    On that chill November day,
The blaze of that orange jacket
    Seemed farther and farther away.

And like those darlings racing
    Across the deep ploughed field,
A flood of thoughts came o'er me,
    And oaths were not concealed.

How often, oh, how often,
    In the days that had gone by,
I had stood on that bridge by noontide
    For a forward place to try!

How often, oh, how often,
    I had wished that the fox would break,
On the side towards the brickfield,
    So that the rails we should take!

For my mare was hot and restless,
    And my life was free from care ;
Now to see hounds racing from me
    Seemed harder than I could bear.

I saw the long procession,
    Still passing to and fro ;
The young men hot and restless,
    And the old subdued and slow.

Then I gave one word of warning
    To the sportsmen in the wood,
And set the mare a racing
    As hard as e'er she could.

Luckily a ringing fox enabled us to nick in as they came back to Bricket, but they did not kill their fox, though they marked one to ground in High Elms Park.

On December 1, the Hertfordshire met at Bricket in a hard frost and thick fog, when no one seemed to know what they really did.

On December 6, in snow and frost the Berkhampstead Buckhounds met at Cuckman's, raced a hind to Leavesden Asylum, where the whips were pelted with potatoes by the inmates; so the deer broke away and was again taken, after a lot of hard work, through Bricket to High Elms—a day that will never be forgotten by those who saw the fun.

On December 22, the Hertfordshire were there again with a very large holiday field, so did not have much sport, but plenty of fun for old stagers to watch the vagaries of schoolboys out on ponies.

On January 15, the O.B.H. met at Munden, but out of a very large field very few got away to enjoy a never-to-be-forgotten run. From the famous bridge we viewed a great big fox crossing the railway, but there was another in the scrubs which some hounds ran into, but while the huntsman and field stayed for the obsequies fourteen couples went away through Colonel Bigg's Park and Burston's, racing to Cuckman's, where the whip tried in vain to stop them, and they raced through Park Wood, Birch Wood, and Pre Wood, into Gorhambury Park, and killed in the open after fifty minutes as pretty as any one ever saw—at least, so say the lucky fourteen of us who saw it. When we all got together again hounds chopped a fox in Serge Hill and went home with a least of masks; but one of them hangs up now, facing the writer, and perhaps returns his smile at the reminiscences that he brings to mind.

On the 17th the Berkhampstead Buckhounds met at Cuckman's to draw for an outlying stag that had been left out by another pack, but, finding nothing, except a little doe that had strayed from Gorhambury into Park Wood, the worthy master enlarged a deer near Abbot's Langley, and after a severe run over heavy country round St. Alban's and Bricket took him at Bedmont.

During the season 1883—1884 the first morning with the O.B.H. at Munden, on September 28, gave capital sport in the Scrubs, where Bob Worrall brought a strong cub to hand after an hour's dusting.

On October 22, the Hertfordshire met at Bricket Wood, but Mr. Hibbert having a shooting party, hounds were taken to Cuckman's, where Ward soon found a fox in Park Wood, hounds running hard towards Bricket, so were stopped and taken back to Pre Wood; but there was no further sport to record.

On November 5, the O.B.H. had a hard day from Munden round about Bricket without scent enough to kill a fox. The Hertfordshire met at Bricket on December 21, one of the saddest days to all old members of the hunt, for it brought grief to our veteran huntsman Bob Ward, and we have not heard his cheery voice with hounds since. They found a fox in Bricket and ran him to ground on the railway near Kite's, so Mr. Hibbert, who was on foot owing to an accident, superintended the sappers and miners, who soon had him out and hounds reaped their reward. From Serge Hill coverts a brace went away, Ward on the Priest, jumping out with his hounds, but the horse slipped at the drop and went on alone in wake of the hounds, leaving his rider senseless. We who were nearest picked him up, while Bob Worrall, who was out for a holdiay as usual when the Hertfordshire met at Bricket, helped Charles to stop hounds. Mr. Solly sent his carriage to take Ward home, when sufficiently recovered, and Charles took the horn to find another fox; but the heart was out of us and we did not care much for hunting, though hounds did their best to catch a fox, and on returning home to think it all over tears may be excused if they ran down hardened cheeks, for we had seen perhaps the last of a dear old friend and one of the best huntsmen that ever carried a horn. Show his equal and we will try to follow him.

On January 2 the Berkhampstead Buckhounds met at Mr. Bailey's, Cuckman's, and the worthy master gave his followers such a run by Park Wood to Serge Hill, Bedmont, The Hyde, Abbot's Hill, nearly to Hemel Hempsted, round to Leverstock Green, and alongside the railway to Redbourne, Hammond's End, Harpenden Common, Childwick, Hawkswick, to the Pre and Gorhambury Fish Ponds, where they viewed their stag and took him at Shafford Mill, after a run of two hours and fifty minutes, through deep ground which told its tale on horses, for two at least never came out again.

On January 7 the Old Berkeley met at Shendish and found a fox at Abbot's Hill, which led them at a great pace by Chamber's Bury to Blackwater, and Furzen Fields to Pre Wood, across Gorhambury Park to the Shrubbery, and killed him by the front door after one hour and ten minutes. Trotted to Serge Hill and Bricket, where they found in the thick brambles, ran through Black Green Wood to the strong covert beyond the Toll Bar, where, being headed, he came back through Burston's, and made his point by the Noke towards Serge Hill, but was viewed and killed near Waterdell, after forty-two minutes' as good hunting as any one would wish to see.

February 6 gave one of the severest runs ever seen through Bricket, or perhaps across country, in Hertfordshire. The Berkhampstead met at Haxter's End, a railway bridge between Berkhampstead and Boxmoor, and Mr. Rawle laid his little ladies on to a stag that went away from Mr. Williamson's Bottom Farm near Berkhampstead.

They raced up and down the steep valleys by Whelpley Hill, Bourne Grove, Westbrook-Hay, Shendish, Scatterall's, Langley Bury, crossing the London road, canal, and railway at Hunton Bridge, where they checked after fifty minutes. On across Lord Rokeby's, by the Gullet and Garston's to Bricket, straight through the Scrubs, where some one rode up alongside, in the deep-holding sides: "Call this dear old Bricket, do you? D—d old Bricket! I say." But we who knew the way smiled benignly, while others struggled in our wake across Munden, through the river, up to Aldenham, over the grass to Boreham Wood, Furze Hill, Arkeley, Barnet, Maze Lane, across the grass valley to Totteridge, where we took him, after a run of two hours and fifty minutes, in which hounds ran twenty miles as the crow flies, and nearer thirty the way they went. Out of twenty who started with them, seven horsemen saw the stag taken, including the Master and his staff.

On the 20th they met at Harpenden Common, and ran hard to St. Alban's, then across Gorhambury to Pre Wood, Park Wood, Cuckman's Burston's, into Bricket; then round by Park Street and St. Julian's, into Pre Wood again; and took

"DEAR OLD BRICKET."

their deer near Shafford Mill, after one hour and thirty-five minutes, mostly at racing pace.

On the 22nd, the Hertfordshire met at Bricket Wood, with Charles Harris hunting the lady pack. They found in Black Green Wood, and ran to the Toll Bar, where he was headed, and Charles hit him off in Col. Bigg's Park, ran through Burston's to Park Street and Hedge's Farm, where he saved his brush. They found another in Birch Wood, ran by Maiden Crouch to the Beech Tree, round by Bottom Farm to Gorhambury Park, away by Kettlewells and Hog Lane to Dean End, down to Redbourne Mill, where he was viewed up to Flower's Farm, and hunted to Revel End, across Holtsmore End Green to Hay Wood and Tag's End nearly to Flamstead, turned across Flamsteadbury, down to Redbourne and Harpendenbury into Knott Wood and Rothampstead Park, where hounds were stopped at dark, after running two hours. The best day of that season.

On March 10 the Old Berkeley had a twelve o'clock meet at Munden, and killed a fox after a short gallop in Bricket Wood.

On September 23, 1884, the Old Berkeley opened the ball at Munden at 6.30, and soon found in Bricket, where they killed a strong cub after an hour of good hound work.

On November 24 they met at Munden, where a large field assembled to welcome Mr. Hibbert's bride to her southern home. Cold snow showers spoiled scent, but they killed a fox in the morning, and had a sharp gallop in the afternoon from Long Wood to Serge Hill, where the earths had been opened.

On December 5 the Hertfordshire met at Bricket, and found in Blackboy Wood, running to Cuckman's, Park Wood, round Birch Wood, through Park Wood again, and St. Julian's to ground near Park Street Station. Found another in Blackwater, and ran to ground in Abbot's Hill late in the afternoon.

The run of the season with the Old Berkeley was on January 19th, when they met at Mr. Charles Barnett's, Edge Grove, Aldenham. They found a brace of foxes in one of Mr. Durrant's coverts at High Commons, raced over the grass by Shenley, below Porter's, by Colney Chapel, to Stroud Wood, round by Hedge's to Burston's, and into Bricket, where he went to ground, but made his way through a long drain, and was viewed, stiff and stark, crawling towards Waterdell, so Bob Worrall's nippy ladies reaped their well-earned reward after a run of an hour and fifteen minutes, during which very few of the field stood up all the time.

They had another red letter day on the 31st in spite of the gale and soaking rain, in which no one would have thought possible for scent to serve hounds. A great gaunt varmint was viewed across the railway by sharp eyes from the bridge and hounds came to the holloa, settling to his line as if tied to it; so drove him straight to the open by Garston's to Serge Hill and Bedmont, to Gorhambury Park, where they caught view and raced nearly to Redbourne, turned up across Mr. George's to Cherry Tree Farm, nearly to Hemel Hempstead, turned to Megdell Farm and viewed their fox close before them; but a fresh one jumped up in view from a hedgerow and, with the pack close at his brush, ran to ground in Flux Bushes just outside Gorhambury Park, after hounds had been running altogether one hour and forty-five minutes. Even one of Walding's best scarlet coats was soaked through that day.

On February 6 the Hertfordshire met at Bricket Wood and had capital sport with, no doubt, the same foxes, for one was run to ground close to Munden and another went from Pre Wood to Redbourne and back to ground in Pre Wood.

On March 4 the Berkhampstead Buckhounds met at Holtsmore End, ran across Flamsteadbury, past Redbourne by Harpenden Bury to Knott Wood, where they lost most of their field at the railway, and raced with a few knowing old stagers across Rothampstead Park, Hammond's End, Beeson's End, Shafford Mill, The Pre, St. Stephen's, Cuckman's, Park Street, and through Bricket to Waterdell Farm, where they took their stag after a good hunting run which was seen by a very select few.

On March 16 the Old Berkeley had a long draw from Munden, round Bricket, and when they found a fox there was no scent to hunt him.

The same on the 30th; when the Hertfordshire met at Gorhambury they could only hunt very slowly to Bricket, but in the afternoon had a nice little gallop round Gorhambury without a kill.

So ends the history of dear old Bricket up to the present; but the covert is still there and reports are satisfactory, so every sportsman hopes that the two new Masters will have luck and open seasons to show sport from this grand old covert.

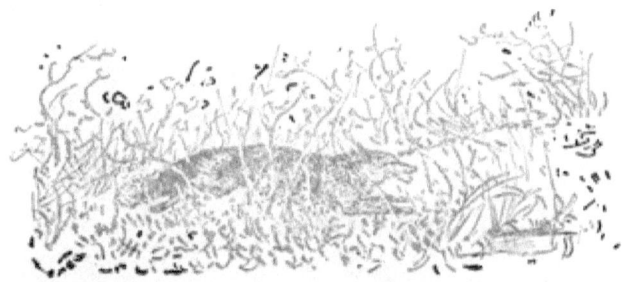

THE RUN OF THE (FESTIVE) SEASON

CHRISTMAS, 1878.

THE RUN OF THE (FESTIVE) SEASON.
CHRISTMAS, 1878.

IT is three weeks now since we have seen a pack of hounds in the field and, if the weather prophets are to be believed, it will be at least three more before we are released from this —— ! —— ! —— —— ! but no, it is wrong to use bad language, for, after all, the frost will do good, although one week of it ought to please anybody, and scent will be all the better when we do start again.

Every Christmas it is my custom to retire to the smoking-room after dinner to enjoy a very old Partaga from a box kept for this especial occasion, and never used on any other unless it is after a good run, when I sit down to write an account of it. It may have been the connection between the two perhaps that set me thinking, but on Christmas night, when settled down as usual in a very happy mood, despite the hard weather, I pulled out my old hunting diary, which is always a source of enjoyment, and began a retrospect of the year 1878. New Year's Eve, that is to say, December 31, 1877, was the first entry that caught my eye. The Hertfordshire Hounds met at Ickleford Gate, near Hitchin, and I was trying to recall some of the principal incidents of the day, which, if I remember right, was a very enjoyable one.

Somehow or other I found myself out with the hounds, riding an old cob, which, though she is a good hack, and often when coming home from dining out, I declare she is the best in England—how is it that they all seem so at that time?—I never rode her hunting in all my life, so what induced me to do so now goodness only knows. Anyhow, there we were. We had boxed down by rail to Harpenden.

It was getting late in the day, and we were somewhere near Hitchin. The field was getting reduced, and the Master gave orders that if we did not find in the next covert, hounds were to go home, when there was a rumour of a brace of foxes having taken up their abode in a small spinney near some cottages, and done some havoc amongst poultry. Faces looked brighter, for, as there were only a few of the right sort left to enjoy the sport, a good run was to be expected.

As luck would have it, my groom came along with the little grey horse, fresh as paint, so it did not take long to change and trot on to the cottages, where Charles, with the hounds round him, was talking to an old woman, while some of the field were poking about in the ruins of an old barn where the foxes had been seen.

"Do kill the varmints, there's a good gentleman. They've took my Christmas turkey."

"All right, old lady, and you saw them in the garden this morning?" said Charles. "Don't make a noise or we shall chop him."

"Will yer trot on to that hedgerow, please, sir, and whip it along?"

Away we went, and out jumped the vixen. One holloa, and the beauties are close at her, down to a lane near a big covert. Confound it! a man standing in the lane headed her short, and she just had time to lie in the ditch while hounds jumped over her, and she sneaked back right to us. We pull up to holloa but hounds rattle into covert, and just before them we see the old dog, who has been running the same line without our having seen him get up. Jumping into covert, I drop my whip—a favourite one—but no time to pick it up, and we rattle along through the covert.

Hulloa! here's a brook, and those boggy sides don't look like safety, but here comes C. W. on his chestnut. He knows the country, and by the confident way he is riding away from hounds it is ten to one he knows a bridge, so we turn down a ride right-handed, from which we can still see hounds running hard.

"Where are you going?" says C. "I don't know," said I, "where's a bridge?" There's Charles with his hounds; he must have jumped it, but there is Jem, too, on my old mare. So he must have found a bridge, but we haven't passed one, and can't go back now. It looks all right here, and is not so big as the water at a show, and we can do that. Here goes! Well done, little horse! It is a peculiarity with this horse always to give himself a little shake after jumping a big place; whether it is laughter, or just to see if he is all right, I do not know, but he did not omit it on this occasion. Where are the hounds now? They have turned in covert, and are clean out of sight and hearing; nor on reaching the open can I see or hear anything. What is this dark crimson stain on my scarlet? Blood! which is it, horse or man? oh, it is only a scratch on the face coming down the covert; but how it seems to hurt now, like a burn. Here's a pretty go! hounds gone away, and not a soul in sight. So let's gallop on in the most likely direction. Where are we? that covert we just left must be Roaring Meg; but there is High Down, and that house in the hollow looks like Wellbury, but they can't all be so close together. How jumbled up the country seems. There goes a horseman over the hill, so that's all right. We are galloping along with an easy, thoroughbred swing for some distance till we come to an awful fence at the bottom. Now I know where we are. Whatever possessed me to come this way, knowing that it is nearly a mile long and quite unjumpable? What is this stealing along towards me over the ridges on the opposite hill? the fox, by all that's beautiful! He must have run a ring, and is coming back to his old haunt. Now, if he only comes on through the fence without seeing me, what a bit of luck. A clump of trees that I never noticed before—they must have sprung up on purpose—afforded me a shelter. Stand still, horse! There he comes in that quiet, confidential way in which a fox always travels, one eye and ear forward and the other back. He comes through the fence and close up to me. What a splendid brush! I shall know what to do with that. Now for a holloa to quicken him on his way; but my tongue sticks to the mouth, and refuses to open. A good job too most men

NO WHIP, NO VOICE, NO HORN!

will say; for here come the hounds hunting beautifully, and we have a full view of them while sitting there waiting. As they come nearer I can make out Layman and Limner leading; there is old Myrtle, too, I thought she was dead; and that unrounded one must be my own beautiful puppy. But I know he is dead three weeks ago. How did he get here? But now they are scrambling through the hedge, so we will turn our heads the right way, and give them a cheer, but it is no use. Hard lines, too, for no one who has been with them can get over the fence, so we have them all to ourselves. No voice, no horn, and no whip! Was ever such bad luck? However they are on good terms with their fox, and seem to glide along like phantoms, while the grey lays himself out again and seems to fly. On we go through the covert. There is no fear of the brook now, we know where to have it and take it easily. Up a ride to the lane they race into the open again, and there stands the old woman, waving her apron.

"He's close before them! they will kill him directly! Here's your whip, sir."

"Well done, mother! here's a sovereign to get another turkey."

A young farmer on a bay colt cuts in just at the nick of time.

Yonder he goes through the rails into the garden.

Tally-ho! Forrard you beauties, we never fear timber with you. Come up, hoss! Well done again; if your mistress could only see you now! There is a crash behind as the colt comes through. We ought to have let him go first and save us the trouble; it is no good looking back, for we can't be bothered with loose horses now, and the old woman will look to them. Tally-ho! tally-ho! they catch a view and race him. Loo! Loo! Loo! Who-whoop! they've got him. I jump from my horse and get him by the scruff of the neck to hold him up.

Confound it, he's not dead yet. What makes him squeak so? and I'll be hanged if he is not licking my face.

Whether any of the field came up I do not know, for I woke up and found I had laid hold of my favourite fox-terrier, who had been lying on my knee, and expressing her indignation at being so rudely disturbed. Luckily it was her master and no one else, or she would not have been content with licking their face. Although this has taken some time to write it did not take long to dream, for on waking I found the cigar which had dropped from my hand, and inflicted a slight burn on the chin, no doubt when I lost my whip, was still alight. Hunting news is scarce this week, as no hounds have been out. So, as I have enjoyed such a run, and accounted for a fox, single-handed, without the risk of riding to hounds, I give an account of it as it happened. Having spent a pleasant Christmas in spite of the weather, I hope all other good sportsmen have done the same, and wish them a happy New Year and open weather.

P.S.—Horray! if it isn't a thaw this morning, and there is a chance of our getting out with hounds again this year, which we did.

HUNT SUBSCRIPTIONS.

HUNT SUBSCRIPTIONS.

A FEW words on the above subject will not come amiss, and at the same time will draw the attention of readers to an evil which I am sorry to say is yearly on the increase. This year especially the cry of hard times offers an extra excuse, and in several countries I am sorry to hear complaints of shortness of money and difficulty in raising the required funds, whilst fears are already expressed that sport will have to be curtailed in proportion. This is not as it should be, for in spite of hard times and general cutting down of expenditure, hunting should be the very last to suffer. There is no need here to say anything about its advantages, but it would be a very bad day for this country if hunting were to be given up, and all the sportsmen who form the backbone of England's greatness were driven to seek their pursuits in other climes. There is not much fear of this at present, for there is no falling off in the number of packs kept. Private packs and those kept up entirely at the expense of the Master number about twelve, and all honour is due to those noblemen and gentlemen who generously keep up princely establishments to provide sport for the benefit of their country. With them at present we have nothing to do; it is with the subscription packs, where the Master is to a great extent dependent on his followers for support. The old idea of a Master living out of his hounds is a thing of the past, for no one nowadays ever undertakes the Mastership of a pack without ample private means which he is willing to devote to make up all deficiencies in the hunt, besides a largely increased outlay on his own account; but this is no reason why the subscription lists should be allowed to fall off, as they so often do when Master and Treasurer are too easy-going.

With a subscription pack the office of secretary and treasurer is almost, if not quite, as important as that of Master, for while one is responsible for the sport in the field, and all belonging to the management, the other has to find the means wherewith to carry it on; and in some countries, especially those near town, this is by no means an agreeable post. A sportsman, whether he lives in the country or only runs down from town to hunt, gives the treasurer no trouble. These pay their subscriptions liberally and punctually at the beginning of the season, knowing what obligations they are under to others who provide sport and find land for them to ride over. But in every country there are a lot of shufflers,

Patent screws, or as a very irate treasurer once remarked over an incorrigible, "Can't find a word bad enough for them; but call them what you like, darn them—they are all alike, and only one place fit to hold them." The excuses these make when the treasurer calls on them would be ludicrous sometimes were it not for the evil it brings about. When a man subscribes to a hunt he identifies himself with it, and is careful to keep up its reputation; but those who subscribe nothing have no identity, and do not care what they do, so it is just ten to one if needless damage is committed it is one of these who is the culprit. There is a large class of shufflers living in every country who pass for good fellows, and every one thinks that they subscribe to the hounds, yet they manage somehow or other to evade the treasurer. They promise to pay, and even put down their names, but get out on some excuse or other; and if they happen to own a covert or two, or perhaps have a little influence, the Master puts up with the loss sooner than make a row. Often the excuse is, "Oh, the Master is a rich man; why should a poor man like me subscribe for his pleasure?" No one knows this but the Master and treasurer, so the shuffler is enabled to keep an extra horse or two at the expense of the country, so to speak; and this goes on till, perhaps, there comes a change of Master, and all have to put their shoulders to the wheel to find a good one. The shuffler grumbles at having to put his hand in his own pocket; but now is the treasurer's opportunity. He is Master *pro tem.*, and if he is half sharp he will not only have his year's payment, but, fearing no consequences, he may even obtain arrears by threatening exposure. In this way a new Master often finds a big subscription list, with no end of promises and even guarantees. So he enters on his duties with a light heart. He likes the hounds, takes great interest in them, lays out money accordingly to improve them as much as possible, takes a house in the neighbourhood, and being, of course, well received, he entertains in return, and lives well up to his income, trusting to the subscription to keep the hounds. When the season begins all seems to go well. Invitations come in for the Master to dine and sleep the night before meeting in outlying districts. The hounds are extensively patronised by the local gentry; but with a few exceptions there it ends. Money is not forthcoming, and too often, we fear, it is the fault of the treasurer, who does not do his duty towards the hunt, failing to compel those who come out with them to subscribe in proportion. We are not speaking of the farmers, for of course they who find the land should never be asked for a subscription towards the hounds, and it would be hard lines on our best friends if they could not have their sport for nothing. It is the shufflers of all classes who are constantly out hunting, without ever subscribing to hounds, that I would censure and if possible bring to shame.

The country shuffler is bad enough, but the real pests of the hunting field are those individuals who keep a horse or two and hunt from town. The rail takes them anywhere, so when one country gets too hot another is open to them. They generally hunt in couples, and sometimes in gangs, when the nuisance becomes intolerable. Having no interest in any hunt, they do not care how they behave or what damage they do. The treasurer can do little with them, for when he speaks to them or warns them they shift the scene for a bit, or keep out of his way till hounds are running and he is too occupied to look after them. Now and then they catch a Tartar, however, and get a lesson to remember. Perhaps the Master catches them tripping and makes an example; or, may be, the treasurer gives them a few wholesome home truths before all the field; but best still when a farmer of the right sort gets a hint as to their character and watches his opportunity to give them a caution. What numberless tales could be told of their discomfiture, for no one has any sympathy for them. Now what can be done with them? Why should sportsmen and farmers who keep and support hounds be annoyed and over-ridden by a lot of tinker-tailor fellows who do no good to anybody?

Now every hunt has, or ought to have, its own uniform dress or button; and if the Master would request his supporters to wear it at all times, they would not only be known at home, but their badge would be recognised when on a visit to other hunts. The slovenly fashion of appearing in *mufti* has a good deal to answer for; and as nowadays a treasurer has often great difficulty in knowing his own subscribers, how is he to know other people's? So if a big subscriber to another hunt appears in *mufti*, he must not be surprised to hear a few remarks to which he would not be subject if recognised as a member of a neighbouring hunt. Let it be once known that all subscribers and members of a hunt are to wear a distinctive badge, the treasurers would have little difficulty in spotting strangers, making out a black list of shufflers which they might occasionally compare with one another, and bring the incorrigibles to light. The very worst of the black sheep would not care to be shown up too prominently, and they might soon be brought to see the error of their ways. Far be it from any sportsman to forbid a poor man from following hounds, but all should contribute according to their means.

In conclusion, I would give a word of advice to hunt treasurers. While every one is grumbling and making excuses about hard times, your Master of Hounds is going through the same ordeal. He cannot beg, so on you rests the responsibility of keeping the hunt together. Make every one pay according to his means; and though you will come in for a good deal of abuse from the wrong sort, you know that you have the support and good wishes of all true sportsmen, who always look with distrust on a man who abuses a hunt treasurer.

A LEGITIMATE SWINDLE.

A LEGITIMATE SWINDLE.

As it happened some years ago, and of the principal actors in it one whom we will call old Screwtight is dead, while young Tom Smith has gone abroad, I alone being left to tell the tale, it is no breach of confidence and can harm no one, so I will give it as it occurred, and perhaps the moral may be of service as a caution to others of the *genus* Screwtight. The Blankshire Hounds were then at the zenith of their popularity, and showing such sport as has rarely fallen to the lot of their followers before or since. The Master was a keen sportsman, hunting them himself and doing everything to the best of his ability. He had but one fault—being rather short of money, but, sooner than lose his services, we made up for this by increased subscription, which answered well enough amongst the good fellows in the county; but of course there was some trouble amongst outsiders, especially to keep the field select, so it was necessary to appoint some one as treasurer and secretary to look after these very strictly. The choice fell upon me, and being well backed up by the rest of the field, it was easy enough to collect the money and keep ordinary strangers from coming often without subscribing. However, with old Screwtight it was no go. Though of course cold-shouldered by all, the old beggar had no conscience, and with a hide like a rhinoceros no dunning or bullying would ever draw him. He would just leave us for a bit and visit other packs in the same way, then drop down on us again; so we treated him with contempt and left him alone. There was no excuse for him, for he was a rich man and gave long prices for his horses or anything for his own benefit and comfort; so when he came to ask if I knew of a horse to suit him he gave me a chance, which of course I did not let slip. The "crack" rider of the hunt was Tom Smith, a young farmer who bought all the incorrigibles in the county, made them into hunters by his fine riding, and generally sold them at a considerable profit. It happened just then that he had an unusually good-looking one on hand. Our Master had bought it cheap enough at Tattersall's some time before for its looks alone, but finding it had such a temper as to be dangerous amongst hounds, neither he nor his servants could manage it, so he sold it to Tom for £25; and under his tuition it was becoming a useful animal to any one who could ride above the average, though not the sort to suit a duffer. It was a good-shaped, long, low bay gelding, six years old, well bred, and a wonderful fencer when in the humour, but the least thing that upset his temper, it took a very good man to make him jump. Luckily Tom was not riding him on this particular day, but when asked about the horse he invited us both over to the farm to lunch next day to see it and have a ride, which we arranged to do. This just suited old Screwtight, who would sponge on any one, and reckoned he would have a pleasant ride and good lunch, whether he bought or not. When he had moved off after the hounds, Tom turned round with a wink.

"What shall I get out of the old beggar? Lord B. offered me £80 for the horse with all faults, but I would not let him have it in case of accidents—he is such a good fellow; but this old Screwtight, we'll make him pay."

"Ask £150," said I, "if he likes the look of the horse, and can ride him at the farm. Then, if he beats you down, as he is sure to do, take £125, and give me £25 for the hunt, which will stop his mouth in case of a row. The horse is well worth £100 to any one who can ride him, and if the old buffer can't do that it isn't your fault."

Tom's farm was about five miles from my place, so next morning I cantered over on a favourite old hunter that would lark anywhere, and never turned his head, so we could give Tom a lead if necessary. Arrived about twelve o'clock, I found old Screwtight already in the stable examining the bay, and evidently pleased with his looks. Tom, booted and spurred as usual, was standing by, throwing in a word now and then, or answering questions as the case might be. Coming out with the excuse to take my horse, he whispered, "Keep him in at luncheon while I slip out and mount, then there won't be a row." Raising his voice, he continued, "We had better

L 2

go in to luncheon and have them out afterwards; don't you think so, Mr. Screwtight?" The ride over had sharpened the old beggar's appetite, as if that were necessary with one of his class, so we plied him well, priming him with old brown sherry till it must have warmed his heart, and he hardly knew himself. I kept him talking so he did not miss Tom, who got a good half hour's start, which enabled him to mount the bay, and give him a drilling before we went out.

Screwtight preferred mounting his own horse first, and seeing the other perform, which just suited Tom, of course, though the bay happened to be in the sweetest possible temper, and behaved as though he was the quietest, best-mannered animal in the kingdom. There was a rare larking ground round the farm, and of course the bay knew every fence. We were soon mounted, and Tom led the way. It is always a great treat to see a good man and horse jumping when they understand one another. Old Screwtight did not jump much himself, but watched the performance with evident pleasure, and we could see he had made up his mind to buy. He mounted him, and even followed me over a flight of hurdles so pleased did he seem. To make a long story short, they soon began to talk about price; and after a lot of higgling, during which more sherry was consumed, old Screwtight gave a cheque for £125, and the horse was to be sent to the Anchor stables, where his groom was at present located. Tom was delighted, never having made so much out of a deal before, so gladly handed over the £25 for the hunt, and laid out the rest in the purchase of two more horses.

A hard frost set in just then, so old Screwtight, having no chance of trying his new purchase with hounds, had to content himself with admiring his fine shape and showing him to his friends at his stables in town, where he had taken his stud

FORTY MILES AN HOUR.

on the first appearance of frost. The first day of hunting he brought him down by train to have a day with us. Now, if there was one thing more than another likely to upset that horse, it was travelling in a box. But when they arrived at the country station, the train being late, he had to hurry to the meet, so there was no time for a row, and luckily there were three or four others for him to follow on the road; but when he arrived at the covert-side and saw the hounds, we could see in a minute that his monkey was up, and only waiting an opportunity for a jolly shine. It soon came, hounds found, and away we went, all riding like schoolboys let out for a holiday after the frost. Old Screwtight, looking the picture of misery, tried in vain to hold him; it was evidently one of his going days, and go he would right up to the hounds as if Tom were still on him; but he soon found his mistake, and getting tired of the loose bucketing seat and heavy hands of his rider, he began his old tricks to get rid of him. Going forty miles an hour at a small fence he stopped short, shooting his rider like a catapult, and followed the hounds alone till they killed. Luckily the old chap fell soft, so was not hurt, and three or four good Samaritans stopped to help him, though he was well known as a screw, so not much sympathy was shown when he told the tale how he had been done by Tom, and that he would return the horse or have the law of him. So, knowing how Tom had paid his subscription for him, they informed him of the fact and shut his mouth. The horse was sent to Tattersall's, and somehow found his way back to Tom's stables, where he soon attained such a reputation, that a noble lord gave £200 for him at Tom's sale before he went abroad.

DRAG HUNTING.

DRAG HUNTING.

"ULLO! What next? The idea of any respectable author devoting his time to such a subject!" is the remark that I fancy will be made by many a sportsman of the old school on reading the above heading, but my object in writing is to show how a pack of hounds may flourish and afford great fun (no one would wish to call it sport) in many a country where game does not exist: and, even if it did, it might be impossible to follow hounds on horseback, unless a line is picked out.

For instance, in the vicinity of towns or places intersected by railways, wire and iron fencing, mines or big woods, and even in some parts of Scotland, amongst mountains, crags, and ravines which no horse could climb, good runs might be enjoyed with a drag, for we can avoid all these, and the line can be taken over a country which, however stiff it may be in the way of fencing, horses can follow hounds without fear of being stopped by impossibilities. Some people would sooner pursue what they call "legitimate sport" in the most impracticable country, and under the most disadvantageous circumstances; but to my mind, fond as I am of all kinds of true hunting stag, fox, or hare, it is poor fun to be stopped by a railway (both gates locked and no bridges) while hounds are in full cry, and probably not see them again until the finish, even if one is lucky enough to get there.

Every year, riding straight to hounds in some countries becomes more and more difficult, so that a man who knows the country with its railways and canals and how to cross them, although he may never jump a fence, often gets on better than the harder riding division, who are liable to be pounded by some obstacle that no horse could possibly get over or through. There is a great deal of prejudice against drag-hunting amongst sportsmen, I know, but though I should be the last to advocate this kind of amusement when good sport is already shown by other packs with which drag-hounds would interfere, I never can see why they should not be established in many countries where hunting men are forced to exist without ever being cheered by the sight or sound of hound and horn. As to prejudice, how many men who don scarlet and go out coffee-housing ever see a fox or care what hounds are doing so long as they can ride about and show themselves?

If any one were ever to mention a drag, these would be the first to condemn the practice, because it would do away with half their show and gossip; but if a drag were laid from a favourite covert, and their hounds dropped in for a good run, they would just watch them away, and settle down to jog along the lanes as usual, picking up accounts of the wonderful run on the way home, and detailing it afterwards as though they had been in the first flight all through, so they would be just as happy.

The drag is by no means a modern invention, as some people think, for in several old sporting books I see mention of drag, or rather trails being laid, chiefly for a lark, or sometimes to enter young hounds, and once it was the means of deciding a great match between two packs of fox-hounds on Newmarket Heath, where no fox could have stood the pace.

Putting aside all prejudice, let me deal with the many advantages which are to be derived from this amusement, which, to say the least, brings hunting in a certain shape within reach of many who would be otherwise unable to enjoy it. In the first place, there is no time spent in drawing coverts, so this is an advantage to men of business with whom time is an object. Then the line may be a short one, over a stiff country at a great pace, like a steeple-chase, to suit a fast set of riders, or, by giving the dragsman more law and proper instructions, he can take them over an easier country at a pace that would suit an old gentleman on a cob, and often show a really good hunting run if properly managed, so that even a huntsman might be deceived if he dropped in with them by accident without knowing what they were running. Checks can be made when necessary by lifting the drag, and all railways, canals, lanes with deep drops, bogs, and impracticable places are avoided by a good man who understands his business, while those cantankerous individuals who exist on a few acres in every country, and object to sport in any shape or form, can be as carefully avoided; and it is as well to give these sort a wide berth at all times, and not tread on their toes. Wheat fields or newly-sown lands can be avoided, and the line kept on the headlands, and no good dragsman would ever cross a field where cattle or sheep were at large, so the damage done by a pack of drag-hounds crossing the country is reduced to a minimum.

Permission is, of course, asked of the landed proprietors and farmers whether hounds may go across their land, and such is the love of sport inherent in the breasts of all true Englishmen that only in a few instances is it ever refused. Of course in such cases the drag does a bit of road-work, or else takes a line across a better sort of neighbour's land without spoiling the run in any way. Another advantage is, that drag-hunting can be followed all the year through if one is so disposed. When the ground is soft enough a line might be taken across commons and rough uncultivated lands, even in June or July, and it is a first-rate way of breaking young horses and getting them used to hounds without the crowd or bustle of the regular season. In this way I have ridden to hounds some few days every month in the year; for when we kept a small pack some years ago, so soon as the grass was cut and carried we used to go out, either on our hacks or young horses, and steal a gallop—round, home, or across a friendly neighbour—at five in the morning, while the dew was on the ground, and all good folks still abed.

Of course, jumping was out of the question, but we always had plenty of that through the season, so it did not matter. We tried our young or unentered hounds, and had rare fun sometimes in these early gallops. Our season began in September or October, whenever the ground was soft and fences clear enough; so, when the regular hunting season commenced, our horses were thoroughly fit to go and stand a day with any hounds.

Let us suppose that a few gentlemen wish to start a pack in a neighbourhood where no hounds exist at present, one of whom is willing to take the management and hunt them, finding his own horses; but the hunt will provide a horse for the kennel huntsman to act as whipper-in. Having obtained permission from the landed proprietors, they find that they will be able to get a line twice a week throughout the season. For this they will require ten couple of hounds, so as to have eight couple in the field and a reserve in case of accident, illness, &c. Nineteen or twenty inch hounds will be found to be the best sizes for the purpose, as bigger hounds get away too fast, while lesser-sized ones cannot get quick enough over big fences, and are apt to be ridden over. Some people think that anything will do to run a drag, so that some kennels contain a ragged scratch lot, consisting of three or four couples, blear-eyed, crooked-legged twenty-four inch foxhounds, two or three of unrounded nineteen inch harriers, and perhaps a few little beagles, which are all expected to run together; but there is no reason why drag-hounds should not be as smart and level as their more sporting brothers, for a good-looking hound costs no more to keep than a bad one, and little more to buy, if a man knows how to get them.

In the spring-time, when all huntsmen are drafting their packs, a good many hounds change hands, so that is the best time to get a good pack together. Many journeys to different kennels, and much time, will be saved by going direct to Wilton, who has always a full kennel of fox-hounds, harriers, and beagles, of all sorts and sizes, from which a level pack of either can soon be chosen to suit any customer. This is not a trade advertisement, for Wilton is known to every master of hounds and huntsman in England and abroad; and he ships large numbers of hounds to foreign ports every year.

Of course proper kennels will be required, with boiling house, meal and flesh houses, sheds, &c., which may be built elaborately, or run up temporarily, according to circumstances; also a stable, with rooms for the kennel huntsman. The next thing will be to engage him. So long as he has a good general knowledge of hounds, how to feed and keep them in health (of course, no one would ever think of breeding from such a pack), that is all that is required. He must be strong, active, and willing, a light weight, good rider, so as to whip in when necessary, though this duty is often undertaken by one of the *field*.

Then a dragsman will have to be found, and this is more difficult than many people would believe. He must be a good runner, of course, and have a thorough knowledge of the country and its inhabitants, with a good eye for a practicable place, and also know whether it is possible for a horse to jump it or not. Some people prefer a man on horseback to take the drag, but this has many objections. In the first place, it cannot be laid so thoroughly while trailed behind a horse, and it has to be lifted at fences, which causes hounds to dwell at them, and baulk horses coming behind them.

Another thing, a man cannot ride so straight in cool blood as with hounds; no matter how clever his horse may be, he is apt to crawl over awkward places, rather than take a fair fly, or even to throw the drag over a big place, and ride round to pick it up again. This I know to my cost, for it was the means of killing the best horse I ever possessed, by falling at a place, thinking that, as the dragsman's horse had jumped it, mine could, but he had ridden round. After that we always had a man afoot, so that if we did not like the place where he had gone we chose another, the same as in regular hunting; if we fell it was our own fault.

The best drag is made of a skin with the fur on it, well rubbed round a foxes' den, which is kept on purpose, the dirtier the better, and then a few drops of oil of aniseed are added every now and then as he goes along. This will be strong enough to last two hours on good scenting days, but of course these vary the same as with hunting animals, and it is only practical experience which will enable our young Master to regulate his runs accordingly. As a rule, an hour's law will give a good man plenty of time to show a run that will give men and horses quite enough to do if the country is at all stiff or the going heavy.

Two or three fresh paunches make a good worry for the finish, at a small cost, and are easily carried. Hounds come together quicker, and are not so likely to run off heel if they see the others tearing, and soon learn to know what " who-oop " means, even without running from scent to view, but if they are constantly run without being rewarded at the finish, they become slack, and of course useless.

The whip's horse must be able to gallop and jump, and of course quiet amongst hounds, as he will have to be always at exercise with them.

The following is an account of the probable outlay in building kennels, buying hounds, &c., also the expenses of keep and working for the year :—

OUTLAY.

	£	s.
Building kennels, benches, yards, fittings, &c.	50	0
Boiling-house, fittings, &c.	30	0
Meal and flesh house	20	0
Stable, two stalls, one loose box, whip's rooms, saddle room	150	0
Ten couple hounds, say £5 per couple	50	0
Horse for whip, say	50	0
Saddlery, clothing, couples, whips	15	0
	£365	0

YEARLY EXPENSES.

	£	s.
Keep of ten couple, at £8, say 3s. per week	80	0
Taxes, hounds and man	8	5
Whip's wages	60	0
Clothes for ditto	10	0
Dragsman, forty days at 10s.	20	0
Scent	1	15
Firing	10	0
Keep of horse	50	0
Saddlery, sundries	10	0
	£250	0

It may cost a few pounds more or less, according to circumstances; but the above will give a pretty good idea, according to my experience. Therefore, if a few gentlemen can give the Master a subscription of £250 a year, he will be able to do it well, and only have extras to pay out of his own pocket.

Like other masters he should always have a sovereign handy in case of emergencies, and never go out hunting without, at least, a pound's worth of loose silver in his pocket. A shilling thrown to a man holding a gate open, will insure its being shut again after all have passed through, and half-a-crown at the time, will mend a gap, and heal a sore place better than ten shillings a month after, when, perhaps, some beasts have gone astray.

To give an instance of this—One morning, early, going out to exercise, I told my boy to start with a drag two miles off, and take a line for home to try some new hounds, while I took a round and worked back that way, to give him law. Laying them on, they ran across one or two fields, but instead of crossing the land of two old ladies, which we generally traversed, the line took me up a lane past their farm, and on for home by our own fields. Blowing up the boy after the worry for road running.

"Please, sir, Mrs. — met me, and said she would pull my ear if I went across her fields, and you are not to go there any more."

Surprised at this from a neighbour, I kennelled up and trotted back to know the reason, for we had always been across there before, without a word. Meeting the old lady on the farm, I questioned her.

"Well," she said, "I don't mind you coming, for your horses always jump; but the last time you came, there was a rough young man on a grey horse knocked a great gap in that fence, and let my pigs out, so my next neighbour pounded them. It cost me 5s. to get them out, and took John nearly all day to find them."

"I am very sorry for that," said I, "but you must let me pay the 5s.; and here, John, is 2s. 6d. for your trouble."

After a little demur, the old lady let me pay it, and I never had any more trouble in that direction.

Now, let us suppose that a young master has managed to get a pack of hounds together, and engaged an efficient whip; by dint of plenty of morning exercise, and a few short drags, he has made them handy and steady, for it must be remembered that a draghound is no use if he is not keen, and of all others they are most prone to run riot. They will sometimes break away, and run a cur dog for miles along the roads, unless under proper control, for he may have been pottering about on the scent, and picked up enough on his feet just to give him a flavour.

Receiving an invitation to meet at some well-known mansion for the opening day, he sends out cards to his subscribers, and all the farmers in the district, giving the place and time of meeting.

As there are no coverts to draw, it matters little at what time they meet, so long as it suits the majority of their supporters, but, as Mr. Jorrocks has it, punctuality is the politeness of princes, so that whatever time is advertised on the cards, it should be strictly kept, and hounds laid on, at the very latest, half an hour after arriving at the meet.

The dragsman, having received instructions as to the line to be taken, starts an hour before, taking care to lay the drag some way from the meet, and not crossing any lane by which hounds are likely to come on their way, or they would break away and spoil the run.

It is not necessary for the huntsman to know the line, and better for him that he should not, but it is as well for the whip to know something of it, so as to stop hounds if they do wrong, and it also enables him to ride so as to save his horse, as he has only one for two days a week.

If the huntsman has a second horse, he can be sent on to some point. No one else riding should know it, or even where the finish is to be, as that leads to racing, and spoils the hounds by riding over them just when they want most to be left alone, and got together at the worry.

Drag-hunting should be conducted in a sportsmanlike manner, and not made a burlesque, as is so often done, and which brings it into disrepute.

Huntsman and whip should be neatly and quietly dressed ; black caps, grey coats, white cords, and brown top boots look like business, but of course that is only a matter of taste.

Arrived at the meet, should there be a luncheon provided, let the field enjoy it ; never get off your horse while amongst hounds, as they are apt to stray away if the huntsman leaves them, and it looks so bad to shut them up in an outhouse. If you require refreshment, sit on your horse and have it brought to you ; you will find your hounds much quieter and handier for it. When time is up and every one ready, trot gently off to where the dragsman has laid it down. Cheer your hounds to draw for the scent, and let them find it ; once they settle, give them room, sit down, and ride like blazes. Ride a bit wide of your hounds, and keep your field in order. No one but the huntsman should be allowed to go within twenty yards of the pack, for even draghounds cannot stand being ridden over, and there are some men who will do their worst to do so. When you get to the finish, jump from your horse, get hold of the worry, and who-oop your hounds well to it, so that all share alike. Take care they do not get on the stale line on the way home, for it will sometimes lay strong for some hours, and whipping them off will do a great deal of harm. Get them home to their kennels as soon as possible, feed them at once, and let them have plenty of straw to keep them warm; for they require just as much care and attention as other hounds, and there is no reason why they should not obtain it. Then they will be fresh and ready to hunt two days a week. Now a few words in conclusion. No man calling himself a sportsman would start a pack of draghounds so as to interfere with any existing pack of stag or foxhounds, nor would any one in his proper senses ever wish to see this kind of amusement substituted for either; but in many parts of this country, and also abroad, where no hounds are to be found at present, if this chapter should be the means of bringing them within reach of good fellows who know how to appreciate them, then it will not have been written in vain.